STORIES OF GREAT NAMES

by Charles Williams

the apocryphile press
BERKELEY, CA
www.apocryphile.org

apocryphile press
BERKELEY, CA

Apocryphile Press
1700 Shattuck Ave #81
Berkeley, CA 94709
www.apocryphile.org

First published by Oxford University Press, 1937.
First Apocryphile edition, 2010.

For sale in the USA only. Sales prohibited in the UK.
Printed in the United States of America.

ISBN 978-1-933993-98-0

PREFACE

THE purpose of this book is to provide brief biographies of certain historical figures whose names have for long been prevalent in English literature. These names are used not only in correct historical allusions but as imaginative ideas; myths, one might almost say, of the English mind. Thus the name of Caesar in any casual phrase is likely to mean a good deal more than the historical figure of Julius Caesar. And Voltaire, to take a quite different example, has come to stand for a great deal more than his actual personal history would perhaps allow.

But although we may justly use their names in this way, it is unwise to allow the mere sound and excitement of such words as Alexander or Wesley to carry us too far away from their historical bases. The imagination of them will not diminish but grow stronger in proportion to the more that we know about them. 'The dreamer and the poet are distinct', as Keats told us in *Hyperion*; poetry thrives on detail and exact information. The exact information given in the following pages is necessarily limited, but it is hoped that the book may for many readers form a useful companion to English literature. The choice of names is, it must be admitted, arbitrary. Others

PREFACE

will be remembered, or will too soon be found. But it may at least be maintained that for an intelligent understanding of hundreds of allusions and phrases some sense of the seven great historical figures here presented is a necessity. It is an accident, but it is a piece of good fortune, in a book intended primarily for India, that the first of those names should stand for a figure common to east and west, the Greek who became more than Greek, the hero of two civilizations, Alexander.

CONTENTS

	PAGE
ALEXANDER	1
JULIUS CAESAR	29
CHARLEMAGNE	66
JOAN OF ARC	87
WILLIAM SHAKESPEARE	112
VOLTAIRE	141
JOHN WESLEY	165
NOTES	193

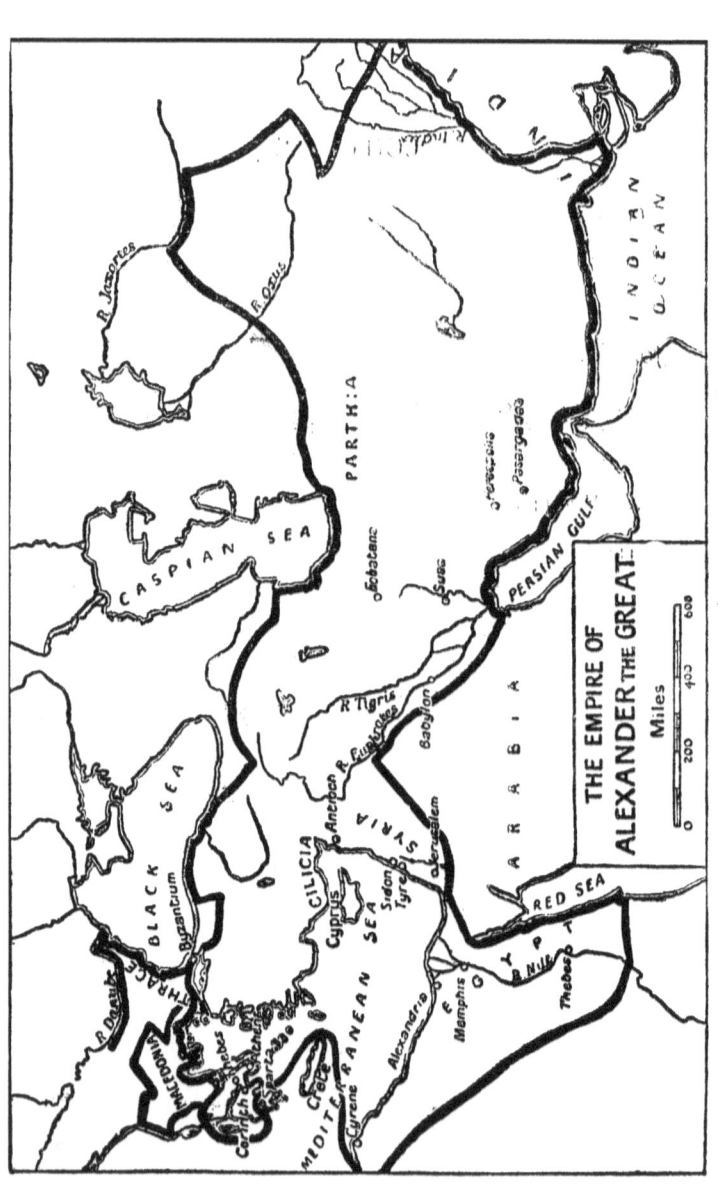

ALEXANDER

THE name of Alexander of Macedon is one of the oldest names of Europe, and one which has had a perpetual fame. It spread over the world in his life-time; it remained a tradition through the classical world when Plutarch in his biographies set it beside the name of Julius Caesar for rival and parallel. After the Roman world had passed and classical learning was hidden, Alexander remained one of the chief subjects for medieval poetry; under the revived learning of the Renaissance it kept its place. The name is in Shakespeare; Dryden wrote a poem on him. In later days Flecker wrote two poems, and a living poet, Mr. Robert Graves, a much better poem.

But he has not been only European. The same name passed over the East, and beyond the routes along which his armies went the rumours of his empire spread. It used to be the custom to regard him as a Greek, and therefore European, king who had made a military raid into Asia and had only turned back on the banks of the Beas at the refusal of his soldiers to follow him farther. But we no longer need regard him as so western and militant a figure. He is, in some sense, a union of the west and the east; he brought and took influence—in art certainly, in philosophy perhaps. His effect and his tradition lasted in Asia as well as in Europe. He stands, a unique figure, between two worlds; there is none like him before or after. The two—even the three—continents that acknowledge

STORIES OF GREAT NAMES

Alexander confess, it may be in spite of themselves, a relation to him and to each other, and if the kings of the East must admit that he defeated their ancestors, the rulers of the West must allow that theirs were no more than unknown barbarians in the days when the great young hero arose in what is now a forgotten people.

He is a union and not a division. He did not even arise in the centre of Greek philosophy and art, Athens; that was left to its own special history, important but, on the whole, European. He approved it, he learned from it; but though he accepted it, he did not belong to it. It is not quite possible to include Alexander in the group of Greek names which do so belong They are mighty, but human in their reputation. Socrates was not deified in Egypt, nor statues of Sophocles offered incense in Syria. It may have been unwise or disingenuous of Alexander to let himself be half-deified, but the very fact distinguishes him. He came from the north to Athens, and the Athenian civilization, spreading with him, changed on the way. The culture of the city Alexandria, for so long the first city in the world for some things, derived rather from that union of west and east which was in Alexander himself. Politics and religions divided and ruined the union, but some notion of it lingered until the Byzantine emperors, who retained something of it, went down at last before the eastern scimitars which refused that union as much as had the two-handed swords of the western crusaders. Neither however could destroy the name of the hero who had almost made them one unity.

He was born in Macedon in the year 356 B.C., the son of its king. Stories were afterwards told that a god

ALEXANDER

had come to his mother Olympias, in the shape of a great serpent, and that her child was semi-divine. His father Philip, however, was himself a very remarkable man, and, could he have begun where Alexander began, might himself have achieved as much as his son. Like Augustus Caesar after him, Alexander moved at first on roads which had already been paved for him. When Philip, ' a man of singular constructive ability and most definite ambition ',[1] came to the throne of Macedon, the states in the Greek peninsula were seriously divided among themselves, and even the threat of their great enemy Persia could not unite them. What they would not or could not do from within was done from without. They could not manage confederation; they were forced into subordination. And the force was Philip of Macedon; his instrument was his Macedonian people. They were, at first, no more than wandering tribes, mostly clad in skins, defending their flocks of sheep against their frontier enemies. So, at least, Alexander afterwards described them, and though he may have underrated their state in order to praise his father's work, yet it seems true that they were the least civilized of all the Greeks; from such rough beginnings came the sudden creation that was to be Alexander's empire. The royal house of Macedon for a hundred years before Alexander attempted to improve the culture of their people; in 359 B.C. Philip ascended the throne.

The education of the Macedonians in manners and in military power, the education of the Greek states in the necessity of forming a unity under Philip, and the

[1] D. G. Hogarth. *The Ancient East.* Butterworth.

education of Alexander in things of the mind and the body thus proceeded contemporaneously. The greatest of the teachers of the young prince was a man whose fame afterwards among philosophers was to be as great as Alexander's among captains and kings—Aristotle. Plato, the other Greek philosopher, was then over seventy; Aristotle was about thirty, with a passion for accurate knowledge, exact definition, and the arrangement of all things in a great pattern of the universe. The eager mind of Alexander throve on such instruction; he received instruction in poetry, in medicine, in politics and metaphysics; he learnt exactness of thought and word and also that universal interest in things which generally accompanies greatness. Yet already everything of the kind was subordinated to another dream. There is a story told of him when he was very young that when news came of some new victory of his father's he was observed never to be very joyous. Questioned, he answered: 'My father is doing everything; he will leave nothing for me.' But his mind was proved to be more than a mere militarist's; he brought to his actions, it was said, 'lofty aspiration, large views, a keen mind, self-control, manliness'. He was never content merely to conquer, he desired an empire indeed, but an empire that should aspire to be philosophy in action, a union of peoples in a humanity of goodwill.

While he was still young he began to be initiated into government. In 340 B.C. he was left as regent in his father's absence, and took advantage of it to overcome certain mountain tribes. In 338 B.C. he came with his father and the Macedonian army to take part in the battle of Chaeronea, where Philip utterly defeated the

ALEXANDER

Greek forces opposed to him and was left the most dominant force in Greece. Alexander was sent to Athens to carry the conqueror's terms, which officially allowed that city free government in its interior affairs, so long as it followed Philip's lead in foreign affairs. Nor was this intention hypocritical on the Macedonian part; it was an expression of a very sincere desire for moderation combined with a very real grasp of the necessities of the situation. And the greatest element in the situation was the great Asian dominion of Persia. In 338 B.C. Philip of Macedon, at the Congress of the Greek states held at Corinth, was named Captain-General of the Greek armies; every Greek was forbidden to make war on him; and all states were to furnish money, men and ships for his campaigns. It was defined what those campaigns were to be—they were to carry against Persia the first war of freedom upon the part of Greece.

At such a point in his history in 336 B.C. in the 47th year of his age, Philip was murdered at a marriage festival by one of his bodyguard. Alexander was then twenty years old, and it seemed not only as if his father's imperial effort had come to a sudden end, but as if owing to family quarrels the throne of Macedon itself would be lost to the heir.

It was proposed to the young king that he should first establish himself at home, and then see what could be done to gain influence abroad. To do so would have meant that Alexander would have to do, or attempt to do, his father's work over again from the beginning, for immediately upon the news of the death of Philip the Greek cities began again to declare their independence,

STORIES OF GREAT NAMES

Thebes and Athens among them. While they were still congratulating themselves on their recovered freedom, the unbelievable news was brought to them that Alexander was already on the march. The resolutions of the city councils had hardly been passed before the feet of the Macedonian regiments were heard on the highroads. The army was suddenly before Thebes, which hastily surrendered and was benevolently forgiven. The King passed on to Corinth, and there was acclaimed and appointed as his father had been. He had taken a double chance, and both ways he had won. Opposition in his own kingdom had been crushed by the measures he had caused to be taken; and the loyalty of his chief general Antipater had given him a power to accompany the power of his own person into Greece. In all military matters of the greatest kind, it has to be remembered that these two powers are equally present. The authority of force never achieves greatness unless the authority of a person goes with it and over it. Mankind must always be faithful to abstract ideas, but all that mankind has ever had or been it owes to certain *men*. The Macedonian phalanx was terrifying, but the face of Alexander was luminous. He emanated power.

It was at that point of power that the familiar story of his interview with Diogenes, another Greek philosopher, is set by the historians. Diogenes lived at Corinth; the Captain-General of the Greeks went to see him, and found him lying in the sun. 'I am the King Alexander.' 'I am the Cynic Diogenes.' 'What can I do for you?' 'Stand from between me and the sun.' 'Ah! if I were not Alexander I should wish to be Diogenes.' The same choice has been expressed in a story condensed to another proverb, *aut Caesar aut nullus*, 'either Caesar or no-one.' Be all or be nothing, such masters seem to say to themselves, and perhaps the greatest are those who do not really mind which.

But Alexander had been created Alexander, and he preferred it. He desired to obtain for his enterprises the blessing of the oracle of Delphi, the most profoundly Greek of all Greek institutions. It was international and unique. He went there; the oracle of Apollo was closed in the dark winter months. It was not to be borne by Alexander, whom gods as well as Greeks must serve. He seized the priestess to compel her to go to her stool of prophecy. She cried out: ' O son, you are irresistible ! ' He released her at the word, either convinced or subtle, or (most likely) both; that cry was accepted and promulgated as the decision and presage of the god.

But there was a little delay while, having established his supremacy, he thought it worth while to attend to his security. He spent some months in making the frontier of Macedonia safe, and in doing so he had the desire to cross the Danube as three centuries later (336 B.C. to 55 B.C.) Caesar was to cross the Rhine,[1] in order to put in sufficient awe the wild peoples on the farther side. He did so, near its mouth, and that river therefore marks his extreme of influence on one side as the Beas marks it on the other. While he was so engaged, the government of Persia, which was now beginning to be seriously disturbed at the prospect of the next few years—not that it expected defeat, but it

[1] See p. 42.

did not want the trouble of victory—was spending money recklessly in order to arouse again the subdued national feelings and jealousies of the Greek states. The great Athenian orator Demosthenes was working on the same side, passionately anti-Macedonian. But the chief rebel city was Thebes, which threw over its pro-Macedonian government, and proclaimed itself free. Within a very few weeks after its establishment the new government heard, and hardly believed, that Alexander, returned at speed from his distant northern wars, was approaching. As he came up to the city, hostilities were begun between the outposts of the armies; battle opened, and as a result Thebes was razed to the ground. One house alone, that of the Greek poet Pindar, was spared.

> The great Emathian conqueror bid spare
> The House of Pindarus

wrote Milton; it was a tribute to poetry not often paid by generals. The descendants of Pindar were the only living Thebans, except for the priests, who were not sold into slavery.

Alexander spared the other Greek cities of the revolt, but he firmly re-established his authority. For now he was free to advance towards the sunrise; the sun of his own hopes was full. He moved forward, as a general certainly, and intending conquest; but also as a humanist, almost as a philosopher. He had a high share of that 'grand curiosity' which lies at the base of all art and science, and his empire, if he could achieve it, was to be as much the union of his men's minds as the subjugation of their bodies.

ALEXANDER

But his first step had to be military. The empire of Persia, two million miles in scope, and having some fifty million inhabitants, had threatened, troubled, and almost conquered the Greeks from the beginning of their settlement in their peninsula. It had the power, but it suffered from the weakness commensurate with so vast a body, if that body is not controlled by a genius. Had the rulers been changed, had the Shah Darius been overlord of Greece, and Alexander been Shah of Persia, Greece would have vanished in some casual summer campaign. An incalculable element entered suddenly into the uneasy age-long relations between Persia and Greece; ' the fortune of Alexander '—his genius and the luck that helped his genius. Besides that, in which he himself so firmly believed, he had an army of thirty thousand infantry and five thousand cavalry. It was convenient, but one cannot feel that Alexander regarded it as wholly necessary. It was help which his Fortune gave him—hardly more.

He who carried so great a destiny was then twenty-two years old, moderately tall and well built, athletic and inured to hardships, good to look on. He had a clear skin, ruddy cheeks, and deep set blue eyes, above an aquiline nose, full lips, and well-shaped chin. Over a good forehead rose a mass of golden hair; his eyebrows were thick, but otherwise his face was shaved—it was he who gave that fashion to the West. This was the form of the king who in the year 334 B.C. directed the crossing of the Hellespont—now the Dardanelles—by the Greek army, composed mostly of Macedonians and Thracians, with some five thousand infantry from the other states. symbolical of his title of Captain-General

STORIES OF GREAT NAMES

rather than central to his military force. That depended, largely, on two things—the heavy cavalry of Macedonia and the terrific energy of their charge, and the Macedonian phalanx, a foot formation invented by his father Philip, an unbreakable mass sixteen files deep bristling on all sides with five lines of long spears thrust out in advance of the front rank. These were his chief instruments; over them was himself. As if to renew in his own person the myths of the past he caused the crossing to be made over the channel to the plains where Troy had been supposed to stand, and was the first to leap ashore in full armour on the Asian coast. But though he came as a Greek he came also as a reconciler. He offered sacrifices to the name and shade of Priam, once in those 'battles long ago' the King of Troy, and he ordered the rebuilding and repopulation of the city.

He was never to cross again into Greece; he had gone out to become, as it were, something different from Macedonian king, or Greek Captain-General, or even Asiatic emperor, to be a thing unique, the full Alexander of history and myth. He had, though he did not know it, only eleven years to work in. He was to die at thirty-three in Babylon. Those eleven years divide themselves roughly into four parts:

1. The preliminary victories, 334-33 B.C.
2. The establishment of power, 332-30 B.C.
3. The descent into the East, 330-25 B.C.
4. The return to Babylon, 325-23 B.C.

1. The first two years were spent in the checking of the Persians, and in providing himself with space to

ALEXANDER

move in, by the conquest of Asia Minor. The great difficulty that Alexander had at first was the lack of ships; he had an army but no navy; whereas the Persians had both. The Aegean Sea, between Greece and Asia, had therefore to be regarded as hostile. The first clash between the two armies was on the Granicus where, by the operation of the Macedonian cavalry, a Persian army was completely destroyed. This defeat led to the determination of the Shah Darius III to take the field himself with an army of 100,000 men. But while preparations for this were made, and along the magnificent Persian roads the levies of the Empire marched in towards Susa, the capital, at the order of the Great King, Alexander occupied the western part of Asia Minor, taking the cities, repelling the mountain tribes and establishing a firm Asiatic base. It was from this period that the tale of the 'cutting of the Gordian knot' dates. At Gordium, a city of Phrygia, on one of the great highways, there was in a temple the yoke and pole of a wagon dedicated to the gods, and so curiously fastened together that neither end of the cord could be found nor could the knot be unfastened. Alexander went to see it, and was told that the prophecies declared that whoever could loosen it would hold the rule of Asia. He was unwilling (one tale runs) to leave it unsolved, lest rumour should declare his incapacity for both purposes, and, suddenly drawing his sword, cut the cord so that it fell apart, saying: 'Thus I undo it.'

The next year saw Darius moving northward. The mountains lay between him and the invader, and Alexander refused to cross them, preferring to wait in the more difficult country the approach of the unwieldy army of the Shah rather than to expose his own in the open plains. Darius allowed himself to be persuaded by his satraps into crossing the passes in order to destroy what seemed the barbarian riot which was inconveniencing the Empire. On the banks of the River Issus (north of what is now Alexandretta) the earlier victory was repeated by the Captain-General. He himself led his Macedonian horse to crush the Persian left, then wheeled inward to where the Shah in person occupied a chariot in the centre. The horses, wounded and wild, plunged till they threatened to overturn it, and the Shah was compelled to mount a horse and retreat ; as he did so the whole Persian line broke. The retreat became a rout, the rout a dreadful struggle of fugitive against fugitive as well as against pursuer. Darius, recrossing the mountains, found himself with four thousand men only and fell back on his capital. The Captain-General, passing through the Persian camp, surveyed the riches—the adorned and perfumed furniture of gold, the panoplies and provisions—and said to the companions who were with him : ' This then is royalty ! ' The mother, wife and children of Darius were in the camp, fearful of their lord's death and their own doom. He sent them word of reassurance and protection.

2. This defeat meant that until another imperial levy of men had been raised the Persians could not act. Alexander had opportunity to follow them up : if he chose. But he preferred, wisely, to attend to the uncertain world immediately around and behind him— Syria, Egypt, and the Aegean. He could not defeat the

ALEXANDER

Persian navy at sea, but he could seize or destroy their harbours. With much difficulty and delay he took Tyre; then, moving down the coast, Gaza. Syria thus could offer no refuge to the Persian ships. While he was thus occupied an embassy came from Darius to offer peace, with an indemnity and cession of territory. So good were the terms that Parmenio, one of Alexander's generals, said to the Captain-General: 'I should accept these, if I were Alexander.' 'So should I', his young commander answered, 'if I were Parmenio.' It is a saying which runs with the saying about Diogenes, and it is in some sense a definition of Alexander that he had a kind of splendid irrationality which refused the judgements both of the contemplative philosopher and of the intelligent statesman. He neither rejected the world, nor compromised with the world; he overcame it.

He went on into Egypt, and Egypt, delighted to be free of the Persian supremacy, welcomed him. There at the mouth of the Nile he founded Alexandria, a city which was to become a centre and a port not only for trade and navies, but for intellect and art. It became a place for the gathering of world sciences and world religions; into the crowds of Alexandria dissolved the elements of Alexander its founder. For by now he was leaving his beginnings behind him; he was becoming universal. He had been King of Macedon; he was still Captain-General; but that concept of himself was soon to be outgrown as much as that of the mere Macedonian king. The change was prophesied and symbolized by the visit to the Temple of Jupiter-Ammon.

STORIES OF GREAT NAMES

Over all the near east the thousand gods had gathered to themselves many names from their many tribes of worshippers. The god who was worshipped as Jupiter in Greece and Italy was recognized as one with the Ammon of Asia and Africa. A temple had been raised to him in the remote deserts of North Africa, and it was to this temple that the Captain-General came.

He had marched west from Egypt along the coast of Africa, in order finally to control the seas, and two hundred miles from Alexandria had received the submission of Cyrene, a distant harbour upon the coast, and then he plunged into the desert, a two hundred mile march to the south. There lay the mysterious temple whose fame had reached him, and drawn him from his secular designs. It stood in an oasis among palm trees; and there, alone, he went in and spoke to the priestly custodian. It is said that he asked if vengeance had fallen on his father's murderers, and that the priest answered: 'Speak more humbly; *your* father was no mortal.' Either to him alone, or to him as he came out to his companions, it is said the priest used a phrase of divine implication: 'Son of Zeus,' 'son of Ammon'. It seems true that the visit and dialogue struck to his heart, but its meaning was not necessarily more, even to him, than he already believed. He was not to be measured by Diogenes or Parmenio; he was not to be thought, except by accident, Macedonian or Greek or Oriental. He was Alexander; that Alexander should be the son of a god was not unfitting, but that did not do more than adorn the man himself, the man of conquest, the man of creation, the world-maker, Alexander. He was twenty-five

ALEXANDER

years old ; as he rode back to Egypt he knew that over Greece, Egypt, Syria, Asia Minor, and the Aegean, his power and name were established. Something of his duty as Captain-General remained still to be done ; he moved upward from Egypt to Tyre, and from there he set out on the final grand advance into Persia against the newly-gathered levies of the Shah. It was the year 331 B.C., and he had eight years more to live.

He set out from Tyre, and, marching north-east, crossed the Euphrates, and held on along the northern side of Mesopotamia towards the Tigris, on the other side of which in the broad plain below the mounds of Nineveh the army of Darius lay, a million strong, gathered from all nations and cities that obeyed the Persian rule. It had here all the advantages it had lost in the cramped battle-field by the Issus. The army of Alexander marching over a range of hilly ground came in sight of its enemy in an early September dawn. It was determined not to attack till the field had been reconnoitred, and all day long in vain expectations the Persians stood to arms.

'In this month, about the beginning of the feast of Mysteries at Athens, there was an eclipse of the moon, the eleventh night after which, the two armies being now in view of one another, Darius kept his men in arms, and by torchlight took a general review of them. But Alexander, while his soldiers slept, spent the night before his tent with his diviner Aristander, performing certain mysterious ceremonies, and sacrificing to the god Fear. In the meanwhile the oldest of his commanders, and chiefly Parmenio, when they beheld all the plain between Niphates and the Gordyaean mountains shining with the lights and fires which were made by the barbarians, and heard the uncertain and confused sound of voices out of their camp, like the distant roaring of a vast ocean, were so amazed at the thoughts of such a multitude, that after some conference among themselves, they concluded it an enterprise too difficult and hazardous for them to engage so numerous an enemy in the day, and therefore meeting the king as he came from sacrificing, besought him to attack Darius by night, that the darkness might conceal the danger of the ensuing battle. To this he gave them the celebrated answer, " I will not steal a victory ". After they were gone from him with this answer, he laid himself down in his tent and slept the rest of the night more soundly than was usual with him, to the astonishment of the commanders, who came in to him early in the morning, and were fain themselves to give order that the soldiers should breakfast. But at last, time not giving them leave to wait any longer, Parmenio went to his bedside, and called him twice or thrice by name, till he waked him, and then asked him how it was possible, when he was to fight the most important battle of all, he could sleep as soundly as if he were already victorious. " And are we not so, indeed," replied Alexander, smiling, " since we are at last relieved from the trouble of wandering in pursuit of Darius through a wide and wasted country, hoping in vain that he would fight us ? " [1]

The Macedonian army was only sufficient, with less than fifty thousand men, to cover the enemy's centre. Even of these Alexander held a proportion in reserve,

[1] Plutarch's *Life of Alexander*; trans. by A. H. Clough.

ALEXANDER

in order to thwart any flanking movement by forming the whole army into a hollow square. He himself, leading the cavalry as was his custom, inclined to the right as he advanced, so that eventually he approached the left centre of the Persians. There was heavy cavalry fighting on the extreme Macedonian right, and two hundred scythe-armed chariots were driven against the infantry in their centre. Both these Persian attacks were defeated, but their movement had left a gap in the enemy's centre. Alexander, before his own force was engaged, saw it, and altering direction to the left struck into the gap. His cavalry and his phalanxed infantry plunged full into the Persian army, towards the person of the Shah. The Persians began to give way; the Shah's charioteer himself was wounded; as at Issus, Darius leapt on a horse and rode off, and the uncertain tumult broke after him in a confusion where the only certain thing was the irresistible and triumphant energy of the Macedonian mass.

On the Macedonian left, however, things had gone less well. It was oppressed by the numbers of the Persians; it had lost touch with the centre, and the gap, in its turn, had been filled by a body of enemy horse. These, instead of surrounding the Macedonian left, rode on to the camp of Alexander which lay behind the lines, and commenced to plunder. They were exposed to attack by Alexander's reserve; and presently the battle all along the left hung in dispute. Alexander, fresh from victory in the centre, had brought up his cavalry; Parmenio, who commanded on the left, rallied his own; the second line troops were all engaged. At last the Persians broke and fled. As Alexander galloped up to

Parmenio, he knew that his victory was complete; the battle of Arbela was over.

It was final for Persia. The Shah, flying east, fell into the hands of satraps who were planning for themselves, especially one named Bessus. Darius became first a mere fugitive, and then a captive. Alexander in person followed, as soon as possible, upon his track, but when at last he caught up with him, he found only his dead body, chained, lying in a wagon, while the last horsemen of his murderous escort disappeared in the distance. His last words were to a Greek who first came up to him just before his death. 'Thank Alexander for his care of my mother, my wife and children. I touch his hand through you.' Bessus escaped, to maintain the struggle.

But this conclusion did not take place until after Alexander had entered Babylon, Susa, and other great cities. He seized the treasure and took over the administration of the empire. He proposed no alteration in religion or society, except in so far as his views of justice and order might compel. It was not for him to impose one system instead of another; their union was rather in their general obedience to himself and the order which was Alexandrian. Two incidents—one deliberate, the other (as far as we know) accidental—illuminate the new state of things. He dismissed the forces of the Greek allies which had up to now accompanied him. Those who wished to enlist under him were allowed to do so; those who wished to return had expenses paid and a gratuity. The Captain-General of the Greeks had ended his business; Alexander had only begun his. Men might choose to whom they

ALEXANDER

belonged, and go or stay accordingly. The other incident was the burning, at the end of a revel, it was said, of the Palace of Persepolis, the chief royal house of Persia. It was perhaps a half-drunken accident; perhaps a political exhibition of the triumph of the Greeks. But, deliberate or not, it was consonant with the other act; the disbanded allies and the burned Persian house signified the coming of the world-state, in which all cultures, philosophies, and cities might play a part, having only a common loyalty to bind and reconcile them. The almost forgotten West and the yet unexplored East were to be one.

3. The pursuit of Darius by Alexander opens, in 330 B.C., the third period of his career. This pursuit had brought the army in the direction of the Caspian Sea, which at last they beheld, and supposed to be connected with the Black Sea. Thence he proceeded either to subdue or to receive the submission of the satraps of the extreme provinces. In 339 B.C. he had come as far as the modern Herat, which is the successor of one of his own half-Greek cities, and proceeded to secure the country south of it. It was during this that there came to light a real or supposed conspiracy against his life, to which the son of the general Parmenio was privy. The conservative Macedonian party among his generals and companions had seen with dismay and gloom the growth of the new Alexander. World-empires, for them, meant not unnaturally, Greek, and preferably Macedonian, subjugation of hostile aliens; they did not mean Persian governors confirmed by the supreme ruler, Persian or other officials in the civil service oriental religions recognized and attended,

oriental etiquette accepted at court, and oriental dress, at least in part, adopted on ceremonial occasions, by Alexander himself; in all, a compromise, or perhaps an attempt at union, which signified one thing to its creator but something less, and more hateful, to his old companions. Reports were brought to Alexander which implicated several of the younger men of the 'patriotic' party, including Parmenio's son. He was judged guilty by a court-martial, and afterwards tortured to extract a confession. Apparently satisfied, Alexander, who had been secretly present, not only ordered him to be executed, but sent orders for Parmenio also to be put to death. The command was obeyed by the officers of the army. New faces began to surround the person, as new ideas had been filling the mind, of the King.

The satrap Bessus had retreated from one city to another, but Alexander was determined to destroy the most daring of the Persian 'patriots'. He pushed on after him, and (which was, perhaps, half the attraction) through strange lands, to what are now Kandahar and Kabul, then over the Hindu-Kush up towards Bokhara. On the way he established here and there new colonies, to be the capital cities of his world-culture, Greek in idea and more than Greek in development. When at last he came up with the fugitive Bessus, by then almost as deserted as his master had been, but unfortunately still living, he caused him to be tried by his own countrymen according to Persian law as a traitor to Darius.

The next two years, from 329-7 B.C., were spent in this region of Central Asia. It was a strong part, and occupied by strong nations. Yet here also, at a distance

ALEXANDER

so remote from Macedon and Athens, Alexander established a settled peace and unity with Athens and Babylon, with Memphis and Cyrene. He crushed opposition, he settled colonies and cities (eight, at least), he left so high a tradition of himself that the chieftains of to-day, it is said, claim descent from that semi-divine and stormy apparition. For the time being he accepted the river Jascartes, which had been the boundary of Persia, as his limit. In the midst of this occurred the second tragedy in the relations of Alexander with his friends. It was the year 328 and the King was twenty-eight.

Clitus was one of the commanders of the cavalry. He was a strong pro-Macedonian, but also a strong friend of the King. When he was half-drunk, however, he was apt to shout out his opinions, and on an evening in Samarkand, when the King and his friends had drunk more deeply and talked more wildly than usual, he heard, as he lay on his couch at the feast, strange talk of how Alexander was greater even than the heroes and demi-gods of the old Greek mythology. What had Heracles, what had the divine twins Castor and Pollux, done, to equal Alexander? Nay, what had Philip of Macedon done? or the old Macedonian force—what good were they without Alexander? The new men jeered at the old, and Clitus flung back the taunts. Alexander, trying to ease matters with a jest, said: 'Clitus is standing up for his own cause.' Clitus shouted back: 'You treat me as a coward! you who owed me your life at Granicus! You owe all your success to the blood of those Macedonians at whom your parasites here jeer.' Alexander bade him be quiet.

He answered: 'Oh! free men now must not say what they think! Why do you ask us to your dinners? Stick to your Persian flatterers; they will tell you whatever you want to hear.' The King lost his temper; he caught at his sword, and sprang up, shouting for his guard in the old Macedonian dialect, which he was apt to use in moments of abandonment, and which, with a terrible accuracy, Clitus had provoked. Some of the feasters surrounded the King with entreaties; others dragged Clitus out of the room. But he would not go away; he reeled round to another entrance and Alexander, as he raged among those who were left, saw a curtain lifted, and heard Clitus, standing in the opening, shouting loudly certain lines from the *Andromache* of Euripides :

> In Greece when victories are known
> honour, alas, is never shown
> to those by whom the thing is won
> but only—

The first line of the familiar quotation was hardly spoken when Alexander sprang from his friends, tore a spear from a guardsman and flung it. Clitus fell dead in the doorway, and the King, struck sober by the sight, ran to his side, clutched the spear, and was only prevented by his companions from stabbing himself. His agony lasted for three days, during which he would see no one, and hardly spoke or ate or drank. He knew he had sinned. Alexander was never a self-worshipper; he never lost in dreams of divinity the knowledge that he was man. ' God ', he is reported to have said, during some philosophical discussion, ' is the

ALEXANDER

common father of all, though the greatest men belong to him after a particular manner.'

It was as a man that in 327 B.C. he fell in love—he who had so far been immune from woman's beauty—with the daughter of a Bactrian chief whose mountain castle he had stormed. He took no royal advantage; he made regular approach and proposed marriage. Roxana, the daughter of the chief Oxyartes and of Central Asia, became the wife of him who was once King of Macedon. Nature itself helped to encourage the designs of Alexander; there was a son who might have succeeded to the headship of the world-state, had not nature also slain his father before the child was four and men put him and his mother to death in 311 B.C. lest they should disturb the arrangements of the generals and warring successors of Alexander.

There remained one other great civilization for him to enter—since China was never to be known to him—that mysterious land which lay south of the Hindu-Kush, and had even remained unpenetrated to any serious extent by the Persians, though a certain suzerainty was exercised over a part of the Punjab, and men and elephants from India had taken part in the battle of Arbela. One of the old Greek myths recounted how the vine-god Dionysus had passed in his wanderings through India, and now the time had come for a second procession from the west to enter. The army this time was not of panthers and bacchanals but of marshalled foot and horse, one hundred and twenty thousand strong, so much had it grown since the armed Alexander sprang from his ship on to the plain of Troy. It debouched from the passes in the year 327 B.C., and in the autumn of the year proceeded down the valley of the Kabul River. The summons of the King went out to the rajahs, and some came to welcome him. One part of the army moved down the river, to seize the Khyber and other passes; the rest, led by Alexander, went up by Chitral, and so round to join the other part in the Indus plain. The Greeks recognized in the Hindu deities the characteristics of their own; they read into Hindu words Greek derivations; more certainly, they found again in a northern valley the ivy they had not seen since they left Macedonia years before. Recognition went hand in hand with victory; cities fell and mountain citadels were scaled.

The princes of the land welcomed or accepted the stranger; their chief Taxiles received the newly united army in his city, sending gifts of beasts and money, and a contingent of horse for the army. But beyond the Hydaspes or Jhelum River another prince, Porus, the King of the Paurauwas, was preparing war. His troops manned the bank—an organized, strong, and courageous army, unlikely to break as the troops of Darius had broken. Alexander's last great battle was his most difficult; the Indian rajah caused him more effort and more danger than all the forces of Greece or Persia or Syria had done, save perhaps Tyre. But Tyre had been a siege and not a battle in the open field.

It proved impossible to cross the river in the face of the enemy; but on a stormy night Alexander risked an attempt at crossing some ten miles farther up. The scouts of Porus, discovering it, rode hard to warn their

ALEXANDER

king ; meanwhile the detachments of the invaders struggled along a narrow slippery ford through the deep rushing current. Alexander himself, either while watching the river and his own men crossing, and the bank for any signs of the gathering enemy, or when he was himself thrusting over, in a moment's recollection of the land and civilization of his beginnings, exclaimed, as one of his friends remembered : ' O Athenians, what incredible risks I run for your approval ! ' Athens had opposed, Athens had fought him, but Athens was the very head and symbol of the Greek idea, and even the world-ruler owed homage to the Greek glory that was Athens.

They crossed and formed in line of battle. Alexander had, in modern phrase, ' regained the initiative '. Porus found himself with an enemy on two sides, and was compelled to swing back part of his army from the river bank to meet the new threat ; elephants, chariots, cavalry, and foot spread out across the plain. The elephants were in the centre. Alexander, compelled to avoid charging the great beasts with his horse, struck at the left wing and broke it. The elephants were moved against him, and for a little the Greek line wavered and was thrust back. But the veterans of Alexander's foot recovered themselves, and pressed up ; the long sturdy spears of the phalanx, with their linked shields behind, drove forward ; the heavy cavalry drove the Indian cavalry in upon the massed elephants and infantry ; the crush became unmanageable ; the elephants, trumpeting, began to retreat, ' like ships backing water ' ; some were left riderless or became unmanageable. The rest of Alexander's troops began to cross where they stood and charge in to the battle. It was early afternoon, and the driven crowded mass of the enemy began to split into ruin under the continually repeated blows of the attack. Porus, at last, seeing the battle was lost, allowed himself to give a signal for retreat, and himself turned to withdraw. Alexander saw it, and sent swift messengers to beg him to surrender. Porus at last consented; he dismounted, asked for a drink of water, and then commanded that he should be brought to Alexander. The King rode to meet him, in admiration of his generalship, courage, and bearing. When he came to the rajah, he said : ' Tell me, Porus, how shall I treat you ? ' ' Royally, Alexander.' ' Royally be it ; but what is your royal will ? ' ' Nothing more ; " royally " is enough for all.' It was the meeting of two grandeurs.

On the two sides of the river the King founded two cities—one named Nicaea or Victory ; one Bucephala, after his horse Bucephalus, who had been with him for eighteen years and had died that day. This is now the town of Jalalpur. He established Porus in his old authority, in friendship with himself, gave orders for the building of a fleet by which he might return to his Persian dominions, down the Indus and across the sea, and proceeded to complete the subjugation of the land of the Five Rivers.

4. But when, on the banks of the Hyphasis or Beas, he felt his task to be done, and that his return was now due, he experienced a reluctance to return. He had heard as he moved on, of the land that lay beyond the Punjab, the continent with an age-old civilization, cities innumerable, strength indescribable, abundant in

ALEXANDER

nurture of all kinds. His curiosity raged, his thirst for greater achievements grew, his intellectual capacity desired more and rarer food. The world expanded into further and further challenge ; he desired to answer it. Over the river he saw the mirage of a future, ' more worlds to conquer ', more worlds to explore, know, and gather into his unity. He made ready to cross, and at last the army refused.

He addressed the officers—in vain. He shut himself up in his tent, dreadfully aloof—the army was unhappy but unmoved. He caused sacrifices to be made and omens taken—they were unfavourable. On the third day he submitted ; as it was said in the army, by his men alone had he allowed himself to be conquered. The land of the Ganges was not to fall or to be allied to an invader of Greek origin, except so far (many centuries afterwards) as all Europe may be said to be of Greek origin. The King consented to return ; he embarked in the fleet he had ordered to be built, and the River Ravi received the great Alexander upon its current. The Ravi bore him to the Chenab, the Chenab to the Indus, the Indus to the sea. It was midsummer, 325 B.C. There he left the fleet and began a march along the coast, leaving the ships to follow when the sea was quiet and the wind fair.

The march was among his more terrible experiences. Food and water failed on that desert coast, where was only sand and sea. His men died or were lost in the nine weeks' torment, and it was only a starved and struggling mob, but still led by the King, that at last reached Bander Abbas, at the entrance to the Persian Gulf. There presently the fleet also arrived. By

STORIES OF GREAT NAMES

March 324 B.C., fleet, army, and Alexander were back at Susa.

There he proceeded to govern. He set to work to make his empire 'work'. It was no longer to be the unwieldy mass of old Persia; it was to be a true and flexible organism, allowing movement for all tolerable local customs and characteristics, colouring the whole with all its parts, yet subordinating all its parts to the whole. Methods learnt from Greece and methods discovered elsewhere were to be used together, and the ideal, so far as it could be expressed, was that universal dream of producing what the teacher of Alexander's boyhood, Aristotle, had called 'the magnanimous man'. The state was to be one. The army was to be one: he set in hand the reorganization of the regiments. The government was to be one. At a great feast in Susa he took for another wife the daughter of Darius, and ninety of his generals and friends married other Persian ladies.

At the end of May 323 B.C. he was taken ill, on the eve of a new expedition to Arabia. He intended to depart on 6 June, but by 5 June the fever was increasing and by 8 June it was critical. On the 12th the soldiers heard that he was dead, and some of his veterans forced their way into the Palace. They were admitted to the hall where he lay, and allowed to file past him. He gave his hand to each, and saluted them with his eyes. It was his last action; on the 13th he was dying. His friends asked him to name a successor; he answered faintly: 'For the best.' In the evening he died, at not quite thirty-three years of age.

He had no successor.

JULIUS CAESAR

OF all the names that have meant much to Europe there is perhaps none that has grown so mythical as his. His family name Julius has been given to a method of dividing time itself—' the Julian Calendar '; the name of his house has become the title of the greatest of our monarchs—the German, the Austrian, the Russian rulers of the period before the Great War possessed it in Kaiser and Tsar. The title of Kaiser-i-Hind is derived from it. It is used, in irony or sincerity, as an insult or a tribute to the most astonishing masters of nations to-day, and (however circumstances and conditions have changed) the kind of order which he established in Europe still lives as a more or less desired ideal in many minds.

In fact the work and the fame were shared by two men, with their advisers and servants : Julius Caesar and his adopted son Octavianus Caesar, called Augustus. It was the chance that related two such geniuses which established their power, then and since. But the fount and founder of it was Julius. His murder, which gave his work to Augustus to finish, gave his own life to poetry as well as to history. Dante, the greatest of European poets, imagined the assassins as guilty of the worst of mortal sins ; and Shakespeare, the greatest of English and the all but greatest of European poets, made of his death a play which (in his own poetic chronology) stands at the entrance to the period of the tragedies.

STORIES OF GREAT NAMES

This man lived less than fifty-eight years. He was born the 13th July in the year 102 B.C.; he was assassinated in the year 44 B.C. He was a Roman of Romans, a patrician ' of the bluest blood '. At the time of his birth Rome, which had once been a City-State of Italy, had already risen to the position of a City-Empire. It dominated, by direct rule or by indirect alliances, Spain, part of Gaul, Italy, Greece, the East as far as Parthia and Persia, North Africa. It had fought long wars with its great rival Carthage in Africa, and had emerged at last wholly victorious. Yet the City whose representatives controlled the land and sea of so great a dominion was itself distracted by factions, stained by massacres, and swayed now by mobs and now by tyrants. Nor was the peninsula of Italy, from the Alps to Sicily, in much better state.

The government of Rome had for centuries been that of an aristocratic Republic, modified by necessary concessions to popular representatives. But just before the birth of Caesar this method of government was already strained almost beyond enduring. Economic changes had filled the population of Italy and the populace of Rome with discontent, had enriched the rich and robbed the poor. The popular party demanded from the old aristocracy of the Senate both a larger part in the government and more favourable legislation. Civil war broke out, in which the Senatorial general Sulla was victorious. But the proscription which followed could not annihilate hostility to his settlement, and the peace he seemed to establish was not much more than a suspense of terrifying and terrified expectation. Among those whom Sulla had marked

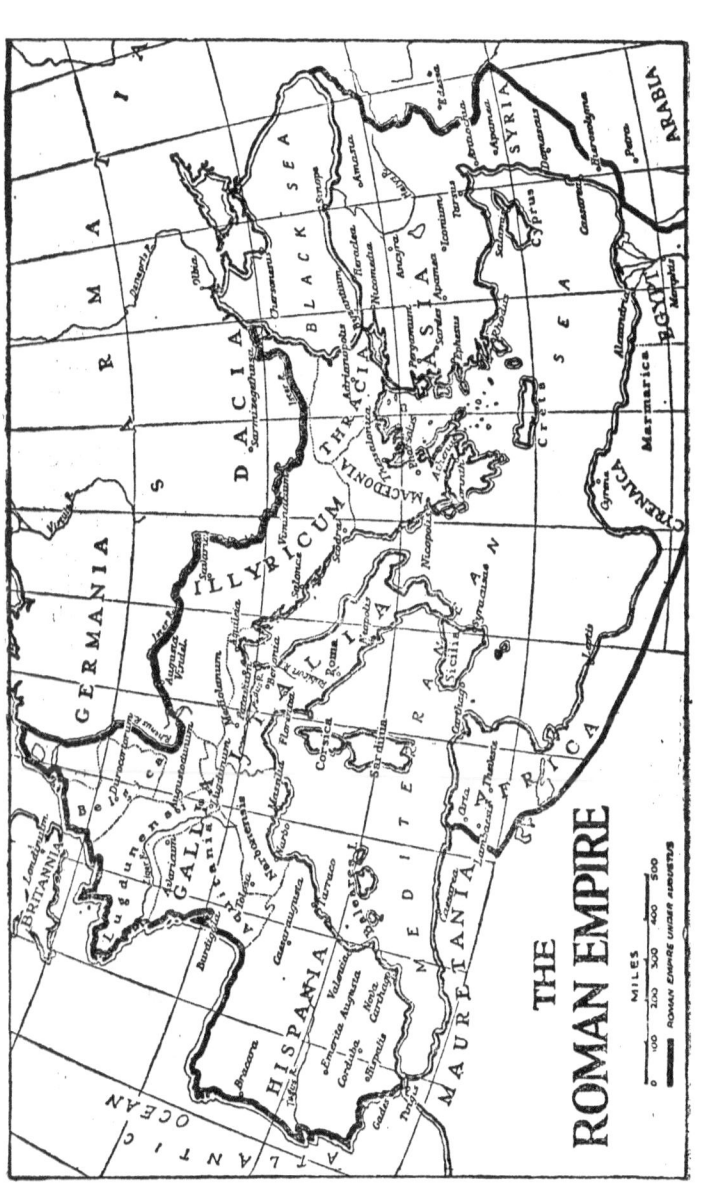

STORIES OF GREAT NAMES

for death was a young nephew-by-marriage of Marius, the general of the popular party, who had himself been married to the daughter of another popular leader. He was caught in his flight, but some of Sulla's friends interceded on his behalf, saying that he was too young, too unimportant, too foppish, to be feared. Sulla gave way, saying : ' Have it your own way, but in that young fop there are many Mariuses.' He was more right than ever he would know ; the youth was Caius Julius Caesar.

It was the natural destiny of any young patrician of Rome to enter public life ; nor was there at that time any careful distinction between civic and military office. The chief magistrates of Rome, called consuls and appointed yearly by the Senate, were expected if necessary to lead armies as well as to administer the state. Victorious generals (having laid down their commands) would be called to civic offices. Governors of provinces were expected not merely to provide and feed but to lead their troops. Arms were part of any man's business, and the mastery of armies part of any magistrate's.

Caesar had received the normal education of his class. Among the few things which we know of his early life is that he wrote verses, afterwards suppressed by Augustus. It was the first effort of that side of his genius which was afterwards to make him one of the great writers of prose. After his narrow escape from a reluctant Sulla, he left Italy for service in the east. He gained a certain small reputation both for capacity and personal bravery. He returned to Rome (Sulla having abdicated power in 79 B.C.) and there he gained

JULIUS CAESAR

another reputation as a speaker in the courts, for this also was the Roman habit ; its public men were lawyers as well as generals and administrators. But their cases were generally political. Returning governors were always liable to be accused by political opponents of high misdemeanours—incompetence, tyranny, corruption. It was normal to the age ; it was the thing which presently was to decide Caesar's own action in his greatest crisis. He gained yet another fame, in the world of fashionable society. He was a leader of ' gilded youth ' ; he made love everywhere ; he made, borrowed, and lavishly spent, money. There were so many like him that it is not surprising public opinion could not believe there was no one like him.

In 75 B.C. he set out for Rhodes to study oratory and rhetoric. On the way his ship was attacked and he captured by pirates. The story told is that his companions were allowed to go and gather the ransom while he was detained as prisoner. He spent the interval joining in the pirates' sports, and on the best terms with them, but telling them that when he was free he would see that they were crucified. The ransom was paid ; he was set free ; he immediately manned ships and literally fulfilled his promise. There was about him already an energy and a detachment. They remained with him always ; we can study his brain but he never showed his heart.

During the next few years he held office in Spain and in Rome itself. He took advantage of the Roman offices to do two things (i) to astonish the populace with the richness of his displays and popular entertainments, (ii) to demonstrate spectacularly that he was upon the side of the popular party. He was a patrician of patricians, but he was already half a demagogue. Certainly this was partly determined for him by his family connexions. But certainly also it accorded with his genius, and was his decision ; it was not a question of principles but of life. His nature could not have lived with the relicts of senatorial incapacity, nor even with those men of lesser and limited genius who were supporting them.

Of those men two must be named—one was Pompey, the victorious general, and Cicero, the rising orator. At this particular time Pompey was away in the Near East, concluding its conquest and its pacification. But Cicero, a provincial by birth, a lawyer by profession, an orator by genius, and a timid, sensitive, intelligent, brilliant man by nature, had already become one of the best-known men in Rome. He was the object of many gibes and sneers from the aristocrats, for by birth he was not only no Roman but definitely middle-class. In the many intrigues of that time, however, the Senatorial party soon began to find their advantage in him. He had a power which was as lucid as Caesar's ; only it was not daemonic. He was a master of words ; Caesar was a master of words and things.

There was a third young man who for a few years became of importance to Rome, a certain Catiline (in full, Lucius Sergius Catilina)—of noble birth, of the worst reputation, heavily in debt. He, like Caesar and Cicero, had come to the time when he wished to hold high office. He stood for the consulship, against Cicero, and failed. Cicero was elected ; a little later Caesar was elected to the office of Chief

JULIUS CAESAR

Pontiff which could be held for life and gave the holder a good deal of indirect political influence. At this time he was working in close collusion with one Crassus, a millionaire and owner of many of the great blocks of working-class dwellings in Rome. The position therefore in the year 63 B.C. was that Cicero, as consul, was supporting and acting on behalf of the older aristocracy and the majority of the Senate ; Catiline, thwarted in his hopes and suffering from the infamy of two prosecutions for conspiracy and murder (though he had been acquitted), was becoming more and more determined to fall back on armed revolt, both to alter the constitution and to improve his own fortunes ; and Caesar was playing a dangerous game of threatening the Government by, without committing himself to, Catiline, while remaining in close alliance with that kind of rich man who would have most to lose by such an outbreak as Catiline was preparing. In his leisure he was still making general love to all the more attractive and more agreeable ladies of Rome.

Caesar, however, was far too intelligent to allow himself to be dragged at Catiline's heels into a general outbreak, both within the city and throughout Italy. He was worshipped by the poor, but there was never a man less inclined to rely on the poor, or, for that matter, to believe in the poor, and certainly he had no use for wild schemes, whether of true or false champions of the poor. As Catiline's schemes grew wilder and more bloody, he detached himself from them, and at last passed on information concerning them to the consul Cicero. Therefore, when at last the conspiracy broke out into open rebellion, Caesar, though under strong suspicion from the aristocratic and Conservative Government, was clear from any proof of complicity. The Catilinian party was crushed, by executions within the city and by battle without. There was something like a scene in the Senate while Caesar was speaking ; stormy crowds came round the meeting-place, and had to be appeased. Caesar remained in office and in influence.

It was at this time that Pompey, then ' the foremost man in the Roman world ', returned to Italy. He had, as was the law, disbanded his army when he landed. But if he was the foremost Roman in glory he was also even more suspect than any other to all sides. There was a general anxiety lest he should attempt to make himself dictator of the Republic. He was flattered and feared. Cicero, Crassus, and Caesar, all made overtures to him. He himself was concerned chiefly to obtain a ratification by the Senate of his land settlements in Asia, but he did not find this easy to obtain. He began to look round, in the midst of the general mistrust, for supporters. Caesar had to take up a government in Spain, but his absence lasted less than a year, though he had to borrow money from Crassus to pay something off his debts before he could leave Rome. It is said that he remarked, concerning them, that if he had a million pounds he would be worth exactly nothing. He went ; he smoothed, settled, and reformed his district, and hurried back to plunge again into the political agitations of Rome. Cicero was trying to persuade both Pompey and the Conservatives to the cause of what we should call moderate reform, and even had hopes of frustrating ' the will for mischief ' in Caesar

JULIUS CAESAR

also. Caesar was standing for the consulship, with the aid of his old backer Crassus, and Pompey supported him on the understanding that he would introduce laws for the settlement of Pompey's veteran soldiers. He was elected. Cicero profoundly distrusted this coalition, but the passive hostility of the Senate to Pompey seemed to leave him no choice. Caesar showed himself friendly; it seemed that the wisest way, for all but the most hardened Conservatives, was to work with the new party.

Caesar, in spite of opposition, proceeded to carry out his programme. He proposed certain laws for land settlement and had them passed. He made some sort of effort to regularize and purify the administration of the provinces. He caused records of what was done in the Senate to be drawn up and posted in the Forum. He gave his daughter Julia in marriage to Pompey. His popularity seems to have waned a little, as usually happens when the Opposition becomes the Government. But he continued to entertain and please the common people with shows, and he was able to force upon the Senate his own appointment, after his year's consulship, to the government of Gaul.

He remained there for seven years, from 58 B.C. to 50 B.C. In that time, it might be said, he not only arranged Gaul; he so arranged it that it became France. He not only imposed upon it the Roman order, but he inspired it with the Roman spirit. But first of all he had to create the very thing he was to inspire. At the time when he left Rome in his travelling carriage, driving at full speed towards his headquarters, the direct rule of the Senate reached only over two Provinces. One lay on the Italian side of the Alps, stretching south as far as the frontiers of Etruria and the little river Rubicon; it was called Cisalpine Gaul. The other, Transalpine Gaul, or, more colloquially, merely ' the Province ', stretched from the Alps to the Rhone and the Pyrenees. The rest of Gaul was still semi-independent and semi-civilized. The rulers were, some of them, called Friends of the Roman People, a distinction conferred on chosen allies; and all the plain of Gaul was beginning to be affected by the grand civilization that had established itself in the Province. But the tribes, whether pro-Rome or anti-Rome—and both feelings were strong—retained their independence. Another enemy than Rome, however, threatened that apparent freedom. The rumour, the news, almost the sound, of movement from beyond the Rhine, came to the ears of the Gauls. The tribes of Germany (as it is now called) were feeling for more room to the west and south. They were beginning to press out against Gaul and the Province alike, and in a little while it would become for the Gauls a necessary choice to which of the two semi-friendly, semi-hostile invaders they should make submission or seek alliance. It was this choice which the military and civic genius of Caesar made inevitable and immediate, which, as he hastened it, he also determined. The finally compacted new and greater province of Gaul arrayed the whole plain on the Roman side. So great a conquest did even more than it seemed to have done, it determined that the dream and tradition of Rome which existed all through her later overthrow from economic delay, administrative collapse, and barbarian pressure should exist throughout

JULIUS CAESAR

Gaul as well as through the south. It was this extra force and energy, therefore, which decided that any later Europe which included France must have the Roman civilization, and all that, then or in the future, went with it as a part of it. This, in the centuries to come, included the Christian religion. It was, therefore, through those centuries, in France as well as in Italy and other parts, that the medieval society which was founded on the Christian idea presently arose. North Germany, and especially Prussia, has never been in the same sense a part of Europe. Nor, it may be added, has England. But England has generally been friendly, and Prussia generally hostile, to the European culture.

Caesar certainly could not have supposed that such great events would depend on his actions, except as any man may believe himself of almost infinite importance. The difference between such men as Caesar and the rest of us is that they are right. It is no wonder that the greatest revolt of the Gauls against his dominion happened in almost the last year of his authority. For it was only then that the final danger of Roman supremacy became utterly clear to the whole of Gaul. Then Caesar showed as a permanent conqueror ; up to then he had been only the greatest—though how much the greatest !—of temporary allies.

It is impossible here to go in detail into the military movements of those years ; a mere summary is all that can be given. The campaign of the first year was directed against the Helvetii, a mass who on the Rhine were threatening the frontiers of the Province. They abandoned any attempt to cross in face of the Roman army, and moving north-west, entered the central plain of Gaul. There, after marches, counter-marches, skirmishes, and perils from uncertain Gallic supporters, Caesar compelled them to stand and give battle. He completely defeated them. After this he marched against another invader, the German tribal leader Ariovistus, who had settled in Alsace and was oppressing the neighbouring Gallic tribes. He overthrew this enemy also, and drove what remained of the broken hordes back across the Rhine. At the end of that year's campaign he had cleared Gaul of Germans.

He had created, however, a new situation for Gaul and Roman alike. Rome rejoiced in the destruction of what was, in effect, a danger real if distant ; the Gauls rejoiced in a new freedom. But nothing could disguise the fact that all this had come about by the creation of a precedent, by the daring of a new thing. No Roman governor of the Province had previously conducted campaigns in Gaul, and their successful achievement had made Caesar's continued presence there a necessity lest the Germans should return, for settlement, for booty, or for revenge. The Roman legions made their winter quarters among the Gauls, and the Gauls realized that the southern saviour was liable to become as certain a domination as the northern danger had been. It was in consequence of this that a confederation of tribes called the Belgae, holding what is now Belgium, began to plot war. In the year 57 Caesar moved against them, outmanœuvred their host, and sent his cavalry to hang on their rearguard during its retreat. Some tribes submitted. But some—and chief of them

JULIUS CAESAR

the Nervii[1]—determined on a fiercer resistance, and fell on the Roman army as it was approaching its camping ground. It was one of the rare occasions on which Caesar was taken by surprise. The legions were disorganized; many fell; a standard was lost. Caesar, snatching a shield, hurried along the line, encouraging, commanding, controlling. He managed to keep the defence intact till fresh forces were hurried up. The fortune of the day changed; the Nervii fled or died. One other tribe defied the conqueror, but as he approached submitted. That same night they changed their minds and treacherously attacked the Roman camp. They were defeated, and their town captured. All who remained of that tribe—fifty-three thousand—were sold into slavery. It was the victorious end of the second year's campaign. The legions went into winter quarters, and the prestige of Caesar spread over all Gaul and far across the Rhine.

There lay to the north-west of Gaul an island called Britain. A certain amount of trade went on between it and Gaul; it was the headquarters of the Druid religion which had spread through Gaul. No Roman general had so far entered, or indeed approached near to it. Curiosity and prestige provoked Caesar to consider an attempt on it, but the attempt could not be the object of the next year's campaign. He had first to subdue more thoroughly than had been done the maritime tribes who became restive under the fear that a Roman subjugation of Britain would interfere

---

[1] Cf. *Julius Caesar*,
>You all do see this mantle; I remember
>The first time ever Caesar put it on
>The day he overcame the Nervii.

STORIES OF GREAT NAMES

with their trade. Roman envoys, sent from Caesar, were detained; preparations were made for war. The country was a difficult coastal district, and Caesar was compelled for the first time to create a navy and fight the decisive battle by sea. The result was the same; and the execution of the tribal councillors who had decreed war and the retention of the envoys taught the Gauls to take care how they laid hands on Caesar's messengers.

The difficulties, however, of this and minor campaigns had occupied the summer of 56, and it was not until 55 that Caesar could look seriously across the sea. Even then he was delayed by another German inroad, and by its consequences. For though he overthrew the Germans, and, provoked by their supposed treachery, caused massacre to follow defeat, sending his horse to cut down even the women and children who had accompanied the host, even that did not seem to him sufficient to put the fear of Rome into the German mind. He determined himself to cross the Rhine, and that not by sending raids of swimmers or by the customary bridge of boats, but as it were in parade and with firm communications for the terrible army. His engineers, driven by that great energy, in ten days constructed, without the help of modern science, a broad strong bridge on piles across the Rhine. The army crossed. The Germans fled into their forests. Caesar extended protection to all who submitted; he destroyed the villages and corn-lands of the recalcitrant. He did not intend to make an attempt at a prolonged invasion. It was sufficient to show in what power he and Rome, should they choose, could make their threat

JULIUS CAESAR

material. The eagles of the Roman standards had flashed in the German clearings; he recalled them, and led the legions back. The bridge he destroyed; it had served his purpose.

He turned to the invasion of Britain. Important as that has seemed to the English, so that some histories seem to suggest that it was the chief and best event in Caesar's life, it must, in fact, be admitted that the two invasions, in 55 and 54 were only interesting minor incidents in the general conquest of Gaul, which itself was only a part of a life that, even during the conquest, was always keeping a part of its attention fixed on events in Rome. Caesar was continually informed of the intrigues and mob-riots proceeding there; he intended to return there with the glory of his victories; perhaps already he foresaw the inevitable close of the political struggles in his own virtual supremacy. In the intervals of manipulating his part in Rome by correspondence and winter-interviews away in Cisalpine Gaul, and of conquering and pacifying Gaul, and of entering and threatening Germany, he spent a little time and trouble on investigating in person that strange land which lay across the Narrow Seas. The test of the historic mind is the realization that Caesar was Caesar and Britain was only Britain. No future readjustment of glory can ever destroy that fact.

He collected ships at what is now Boulogne. He sent one of his captains, Gaius Volusenus, to reconnoitre, and one of the most fascinating vignettes of English history is that of the galley, carrying the Roman staff-officer, running along the British coast, round the North Foreland as far as Deal. Volusenus was absent about five days; he returned with all the information that his general desired, and at the beginning of September 55 B.C. Caesar embarked two legions, the 7th and his favourite 10th, besides archers, slingers, and a small band of cavalry. The attempt at landing was resisted by the Britons on foot and in chariots. The Roman soldiers hesitated, and only the daring (the story is familiar) of the standard-bearer of the 10th incited them. He called to his comrades: 'Come on, men, unless you want the enemy to have the eagle! At any rate I shall have done what Rome and the general have ordered.' He leapt overboard, carrying the eagle high, and went forward. The legionaries leapt after him, and at last managed to achieve some sort of formation and to charge. The first line of our Roman ancestors swept up the beach, and the history of the world was again determined. The stumbling steps of those mailed feet on the shingle meant that England, as well as France, would derive from the Roman tradition.

It is true that neither in this year or the next did Caesar in any sense occupy Britain. His first invasion lasted but a short time, and he did no more than keep his footing and extort a few submissions. He determined, however, to make a grander effort in 54, and indeed he then crossed in July with five legions, besides the auxiliaries and two thousand horse. He fought his way to the Thames, crossed it, and came as far north as the stronghold of his chief opponent Cassivelaunus, perhaps some twenty miles on. He was successful in storming it, but by September he was not unwilling to accept a nominal submission, and to return with

JULIUS CAESAR

prisoners and hostages to the coast, and thence to Gaul.

There the legions were posted in winter quarters. But this great year which had seen the invasion of Germany by a bridge and of Britain by a fleet ended with an outbreak of revolt in Gaul, in which, by the disobedience of one of Caesar's generals, a Roman army was destroyed. This triumph excited the patriotic spirit among the Gauls; the year 53 passed in sporadic fighting, and the next saw a grand rebellion spreading all over the country under a brilliant military leader Vercingetorix. A few tribes had been too heavily and too recently punished by Caesar to risk a new revolt; a few had made agreement with him to which they remained faithful. But in general it may be said that Gaul rose. Caesar himself was nearly cut off from his army; his commissariat was continually threatened; he was compelled to abandon certain operations. It looked at one time as if the Roman power would be entirely lost. But the strategic genius of Caesar, his swiftness of movement, his own personal calm and courage, and the utter devotion of his troops to their general, brought him to victory. Vercingetorix was at last besieged in a fortress called Alesia, which stood almost in the exact middle of Gaul. He sent out an appeal to all the tribes, and a mass of eight thousand horse and two hundred and fifty thousand foot marched to relieve him. This great force, however, did not approach Caesar's lines until the besieged were almost desperate. Attacks on those lines failed. In the last hour of the last effort on the last field the soldiers fighting on both sides looked up and saw the crimson

STORIES OF GREAT NAMES

cloak of the great master of war himself leading his cohorts to the battle. The Gauls broke as night came down; the relief of Alesia had failed. On the next day Vercingetorix surrendered, and was sent to lie in prison at Rome. It was the end of the campaign of 52.

The year 51 was spent in suppressing a few despairing efforts of the last obstinate tribes. It was in one of these that that ruthlessness of Caesar's which had marked his youth was again exhibited. After taking a certain rebellious city he caused the hands of the garrison to be cut off, and sent them away to exist as living examples of the victory of Rome. But by then, and with that, the thing was done. *Gallia quieta est* —' Gaul was quiet.'

The record of the whole business was made by Caesar himself in the Commentaries *De Bello Gallico*, which have served since for students alike of Latin and of war. Cicero and Napoleon admired them; and schools are educated upon them.

' The purity of the Latin, the lucidity, the terseness, and the vigour of the narrative, the skill that excites emotion by virtue of restraint and appeals to admiration by statement of fact without the impertinence of praise, have been generally acclaimed: the critic who reproached Caesar with having failed to recognize the nobleness of Vercingetorix, forgot that he had himself learned to recognize it from Caesar alone.'[1]

All this time, however, while Gaul was compacted Rome was more widely riven into faction and more deeply stained with blood. Pompey had remained in the city, but Pompey had not kept order there. The

[1] Rice Holmes. *The Roman Republic.* Clarendon Press.

JULIUS CAESAR

Senate feared Caesar's reported ambition, but the Senate would not allow to Pompey the power which he half-uncertainly desired. Cicero, still desiring a reformed aristocratic constitution, and making legal efforts towards it, was now friendly and now hostile to each and all. The wilder spirits fought in the Forum and on the roads. At one time, during the winter between the campaigns of 56 and 55, Caesar met Pompey and Crassus at Luca in Transalpine Gaul, and made with them an agreement by which it seemed for awhile that the three might impose their will on the Roman world—by the help of Caesar's legions, Pompey's prestige, and Crassus' money. But it did not last. Corruption and violence spread. ' Republic, Senate, law-courts, are mere ciphers,' wrote Cicero ; ' not one of us has any standing.' At this crisis things were made worse by a great disaster which happened to the Roman arms and destroyed one of the three great men. Crassus had accepted the proconsulate of Syria ; he desired military glory—such as Pompey had and Caesar was gaining. He went to war with the Parthians, and in the year 53, he was utterly defeated and killed. The removal of Crassus tended to bring the other two triumvirs to complete friendship or complete hostility. Rome, owing to murders and riots, was left without a consul. It was already proposed that Pompey should be made dictator in order to save the State, and though the extremer Conservatives would not accept the term, yet it was rather the term than the thing to which they objected. It was the beginning of the year 52, and Caesar, knowing that this danger lay behind him, was marching against Vercingetorix.

STORIES OF GREAT NAMES

The question which was to decide all was, however, no great constitutional principle, but an affair of Caesar's personal security. He knew very well that as soon as his turn of office in Gaul was concluded, efforts would be made to overthrow him altogether by legal charges based on his administration. To avoid this he desired to be allowed to stand for the consulship (and certainly to be elected) in his absence, so that when he returned he should do so as consul and be protected by office from attack for at least a year, during which he could take measures. Pompey had seemed to agree at the meeting at Luca, but now Pompey was throwing over the agreement. Pompey was also (illegally) to be proconsul of Spain, and therefore would have legions to command, whereas Caesar would, at the end of his government, have none. By the year 50 the position was described by one of Cicero's correspondents.

' The point on which the men in power are sure to fight is this : Gnaeus Pompeius has made up his mind not to allow Gaius Caesar to become consul, unless he first hands over his army and provinces ; Caesar is convinced that there is no safety for him if he quits his army. He proposes, however, as a compromise, that both should give up their armies. So their mighty love for each other and their detested alliance has not drifted into secret bickering, but is breaking out into open war. What line I personally should take I cannot conceive—and I have no doubt that making up your mind on this point will worry you too—for between myself and the Pompeians there are ties of good feeling and close connexion, while on the other side it is the cause, not the men that I dislike. . . .

JULIUS CAESAR

'In this quarrel I can see that Gnaeus Pompeius will have on his side the Senate and the judicial body ; that Caesar will be joined by all who have everything to dread and little to hope for ; and that between the armies there is no comparison. On the whole, there is time enough to appraise the resources of both and to choose sides. . . . You want my opinion of the future. Unless one of the two goes to the Parthian war, I see that a tremendous quarrel is impending, which will be decided by the sword and by force. Both are ready, determined, and thoroughly equipped. If only it could be acted without deadly peril, fortune is rehearsing for you a great and enthralling drama.'

Cicero himself wrote to another : ' You ask what is to happen when the consul says, " Your vote, Marcus Tullius ? " I shall answer in a word, " I agree with Gnaeus Pompeius." Nevertheless in private I shall exhort him to keep the peace. . . . On our side every one is doing his utmost to avert an appeal to arms.'

Caesar had distributed his legions in winter quarters throughout Gaul ; he himself, after making a triumphant progress through the Province and being enthusiastically received everywhere, had come south and by the middle of December was at Ravenna. Excitement in Rome reached a climax, and one of the consuls, going formally to Pompey's house, gave him a sword and called on him to march against Caesar with two legions which were immediately available, and to raise further levies. Pompey, ' unless I find a better way', consented. As soon as he heard of this, Caesar gathered the scattered detachments of his nearest legion (the 13th) and sent orders northward that the

8th and 12th should also join him. Cicero later wrote that 'I saw . . . that our friends desired war, whereas Caesar did not desire it, but did not fear it', and again 'a mad passion for fighting had seized even the constitutionalists'.

Caesar made a last effort. He wrote, offering to resign his command if Pompey would do the same, but if this were refused he would be forced to defend his rights and those of the public. There were stormy debates in the Senate, and Pompey moved troops into the city. The chief Caesarians were compelled to leave the Senate House, and 'the ultimate decree' was passed, ordering all magistrates and officers to take action against the public enemy. As soon as the news came to Ravenna Caesar paraded his own legion, addressed the soldiers, set it in motion, and on 11 January in the year 50 B.C. crossed the Rubicon, the river which was the frontier of his province. It was a declaration of war against the Government, and it was so taken. The struggle between Caesar and Republican Rome was to be settled by arms.

Negotiations were still carried on, for indeed the side which had provoked the war was by no means ready to crush the rebel at once. Pompey had never thought it would be possible to defend Rome, and the forces he had at hand, even with any number of new levies, were not likely to make a good showing against Caesar's devoted veterans. He himself, bidding the Senators follow him, moved south to Capua, while Caesar advanced along the eastern coast of Italy, occupying the towns on his road without difficulty. He trapped a general of Pompey's (owing largely to that general's

JULIUS CAESAR

own rashness), and with him a number of notables and some 6,000 men ; another veteran legion joined him from Gaul. His supporters in Italy were raising forces and collecting garrisons. Before this seasoned power Pompey decided to abandon Italy, which he hoped, by controlling the sea, to starve into submission, and to defeat Caesar by superior forces either in Greece or Spain. Caesar quickened his march ; his army moved on the eastern sea-port of Brundisium, where Pompey had retreated, at the rate of twenty miles a day. He reached the town before Pompey had actually embarked, but he did not manage to blockade the harbour in time to prevent his opponent's final departure. Some forces surrendered. In nine weeks Caesar had, without bloodshed, completely mastered Italy; no soldier of Pompey remained there in arms. Cicero records the rise of his reputation for mercy : ' . . . do you see what manner of man he is into whose hands the Republic has fallen ? How clear-sighted, how alert, how thoroughly prepared ! Upon my word, if he refrains from murder and robbery, he will be most worshipped by those who most dreaded him. The inhabitants of the country towns and the small farmers talk to me a good deal. They don't care a straw for anything but their lands, their farmhouses, and their money. And now observe the reaction : the man in whom they once trusted they now dread ; the man whom they dreaded they adore.'

From Brundisium Caesar returned to Rome. He was still in considerable danger. Italy might be quiet, but there was a strong Conservative party who were at worst hostile and at best unreliable. Cicero, for example, whom Caesar particularly desired to gain over, insisted on remaining neutral. They had an interview of which Cicero gave an account to a friend.

'I spoke in such a way as to win his respect rather than his gratitude, and I stuck to my resolution not to go to Rome. We were mistaken in thinking that he would be easy to deal with: I never saw anything less so. He kept saying that my decision amounted to a vote of censure; if I did not come the others would hang back. I remarked that their case was unlike mine. After much discussion he said, "Come then and discuss the question of peace." "At my own discretion?" I asked. "Am I to dictate to you?" said he. "What I shall urge," I said, "will be that the Senate disapproves of any expedition to Spain and of transporting armies to Greece, and," I added, "I shall express much sympathy with Gnaeus." Thereupon he said, "Of course I strongly object to remarks of that kind." "So I supposed," said I, "but I must decline to attend, because I must either speak in this sense and say many things which I could not possibly pass over if I were present, or I must not come at all." The upshot was, as he suggested by way of ending the discussion, that I was to think it over. I couldn't say "No". So we parted. I feel certain therefore that he has no love for me. But I was delighted with myself, which hasn't been the case for some time past.'

Besides this attitude of Cicero and other notables there were greater problems—the feeding of Italy from corn-producing countries oversea, and the enemy armies oversea. Pompey was in Greece, gathering huge forces; some eight other legions of Pompey were in

JULIUS CAESAR

Spain; North Africa was full of Pompey's allies. Caesar determined to secure his base—in the largest sense of the word—before risking campaigns against the greatest of the opposing forces. At Rome by his personal authority he established a government of his friends, and seized the treasure in the public exchequer. The opposition of certain magistrates to this roused him to another threat of ruthlessness; he promised death to any who intervened, adding that it was more difficult to promise than to execute. Yet it was true, as he wrote to Cicero, that he was not by nature cruel; ' it does not disturb me ', he added, ' to hear that those men whom I allowed to go free intend to attack me again. I only want to be true to myself, and let them be—what they are.'

What he had done in Gaul he now proceeded to do again on a greater scale over the Roman world. He had to be at once a soldier and a ruler, to win victories and (under whatever political disguises) to decree laws. In those earlier years he had prosecuted the triumph of Rome abroad, while he watched his own interests in Rome itself. But by now, unless he were to surrender to the view of the extreme Conservatives, which promised no peace to the world, or to that of the Pompeian faction, which promised only proscription and destruction, he must treat his interests and Rome's as one. There is in Caesar as in a few other great men something which seems to make him more than a man. He becomes, as it were, a part of the pattern of things, itself speaking and acting. He has become the world in operation, and the many dangerous chances he had still to take does not alter that strange greatness.

STORIES OF GREAT NAMES

He only just succeeded in being what he was, in doing what he did. But clearly that is true of all history; it was inevitable, and yet it so easily might not have been.

In the year 49 he moved first into Spain, leaving a force to watch the recalcitrant city of Massilia (now Marseilles) on his way round, for he had not sufficient ships to go by sea—Pompey had taken them—and the city threatened his communications. The campaign presented grave difficulties, made greater by Caesar's refusal, on more than one occasion, to annihilate the enemy. His own soldiers cried out against his clemency; they wanted the war to end. But Caesar—it would be truer to say—wanted war to end, he the greatest master of the art. He had spared Gauls; he would spare his countrymen. He desired a peaceful and even a friendly world. Virgil's tremendous line applies to him—that it was the business of Rome *parcere subjectis et debellare superbos*, ' to spare the obedient and overthrow the arrogant '. At last he succeeded in compelling the surrender of the enemy armies, and made a settlement with them. He did not even demand that they should swear allegiance to himself. It was enough for him to conquer, to show clemency, and to be Caesar.

He returned to Rome, Massilia having also fallen, and there, while making final arrangements to pass over into Greece, he caused measures to be taken to settle the economic chaos which then existed in Rome. Credit, in the state of affairs in the city, had been unobtainable; property could not be sold, for no one was willing to buy; debts remained unpaid. Caesar

JULIUS CAESAR

ordained laws which to some extent restored confidence, and the fact that he so acted, and was aiming at a renewal of trust, assisted its restoration. It was therefore as the half-admitted champion of peace and reform, and still more of Rome and Italy, that he proceeded against the combination of Roman and Oriental forces which his senatorial opponents, with Pompey their commander, had gathered against him. The whole position was becoming changed. The rebel was now the defender of the Roman idea. The Conservatives were supported by foreign forces and were threatening massacre should they triumph.

Caesar had had himself made consul, and when he landed in Greece several Pompeian governors were compelled by the populace of their towns to open their gates to the Roman magistrate. He set sail from Italy on 6 November 49 B.C.; the whole campaign lasted till 9 August 48 B.C. Caesar's chief problem was the feeding of his soldiers, in a country where Pompey controlled most of the wheat supplies. At one time, after a good deal of marching and counter-marching, he made an attempt to blockade Pompey in his camp near the modern Albanian capital of Durazzo. Pompey almost permitted this to happen, for he was reluctant to accept the battle Caesar was always offering him. He did not altogether trust his own forces, whereas Caesar was completely sure of his. He waited therefore till Caesar's extended lines of blockade were nearly completed, then by the aid of Gallic deserters he attacked the lines, by sea and land, on two sides at once. Eventually this battle ended in the defeat of a part of Caesar's army, and Caesar was forced to raise the blockade and withdraw. This was in July 48 B.C.

In August, after renewed movement, the hostile armies met again in the Pharsalian plain, which lies in Northern Greece, between Mount Olympus and Thermopylae. Caesar was determined to force a battle ; Pompey, urged by his companions, and relying on his cavalry, consented to accept the challenge. In mid-day of the middle summer the ranks of Caesar charged. Pompey's cavalry, who were intended to take Caesar's army on its right wing and roll it up, found themselves confronted by eight chosen and charging cohorts. They were of mingled nations and uncertain discipline ; they broke and fled. The cohorts swung round on Pompey's left wing ; at the same time Caesar threw in his reserves and broke the centre and right. The Pompeians fled in a mingled mass, but most of them were compelled to surrender. Pompey had opened the battle with 47,000 infantry and 7,000 horse ; Caesar with 22,000 foot and 1,000 horse. At the end of the day at least 6,000 Pompeians had fallen, and 24,000 were prisoners. Caesar had lost some 250 men.

From Greece Pompey fled to Egypt, but when Caesar followed in pursuit, and his galley passed into the harbour of Alexandria, past that red sandstone obelisk which now stands in London under the name of ' Cleopatra's needle ', he was met, even before he had landed, by a messenger from the Egyptian king, or rather from his council, bearing the embalmed head of Pompey who had been stabbed as he set foot on shore. It is said he turned aside and shed tears. But the death

JULIUS CAESAR

of Pompey did not mean the complete extinction of his armed supporters nor the destruction of the Conservative and Republican party. The first was to cost other brief campaigns; the second was to wait until, after Caesar's own murder, it should be finally achieved by Augustus, his adopted son.

Meanwhile the Dictator, so named by the Senate in Rome, lingered in Alexandria. He had resolved, before he returned to Italy, to quiet the east and to secure Egypt against his enemies. Also he had met Cleopatra, then twenty-two years old. But there is nothing to show, then or at any time, that he ever subordinated mind or action to any woman or man. His own word was justified—' Caesar was always Caesar.' There broke out against him a riot which became a war; for some time Caesar, Cleopatra, and their force, were besieged in the palace, harbour, and adjacent buildings and streets. He himself, on one occasion, had to dive from the great mole of the harbour to escape destruction. He remained for some six months in a state of war; then, with the aid of his eastern allies, he defeated the Egyptians at a great battle on the Nile. For another two months after that he seems to have rested —it is the only time when he did. He made a voyage up the Nile, accompanied by Cleopatra. If not the most significant, it is perhaps the most romantic moment of his career, when the ship that carried the creator of a world, and the woman who became a fabulous dream to the world, passed together along the river which has itself been a myth to the world : Caesar, Cleopatra, the Nile. But it was certainly Egyptian civilization—manners, religion, administration—which, as much as its queen, enthralled and provoked the curiosity of the Dictator's mind.

After another short campaign in Asia Minor he returned to Italy. In July 47 B.C. he landed and passed north to Rome. It was not too soon; civil and military disturbances had broken out. But with his coming open opposition all but ceased; the world, as it were, fell quiet. The famous story of the mutinous legions belongs to this period. Those in Italy had got out of hand, demanding promised prize-money and to be disbanded. Caesar met them outside Rome. They shouted their demands. He answered at once: ' I disband you; what I promised you I will give when I have ended my conquests by the help of other men.' He was urged by his friends to say something more, and more gentle, to his old veterans. He began again: ' Citizens,—.' It was a civic word, no longer the ' Soldiers ' of a General to his men. He was interrupted by a clamour of repudiation; he was begged to do anything, to punish them, only not to go from them and not to send them from him. At their passionate request he consented; he pardoned them and received them again to his service. He was always Caesar; he did not forget—the ringleaders of the meeting were punished at a later day.

Similarly, on the civil side, he refused to yield to that clamour for the repudiation of all debts and for the release from the obligation of paying rent which the wilder revolutionaries were making. He declared that he himself was in debt and would not deny his engagements. He did, however, introduce certain measures which lightened the extra financial burdens imposed

JULIUS CAESAR

by the state of war between himself and Pompey. Having re-established comparative quiet in the city he proceeded on a campaign in North Africa, where Cato, the famous republican and moralist who had always been his enemy, on both political and moral grounds, was making head against him.

The campaign lasted from 11 October 47 B.C. to 22 March 46 B.C. Caesar met there ' the ablest of his pupils' Labienus, who had served under him in Gaul, but all the pupil had learnt from his master did not make him equal to his master. Cato was shut up in Utica, and committed suicide as the city fell. It is true that on several occasions Caesar and his army were in serious danger, both from the hostile forces and from famine. But he, like all great commanders, seemed to have an insight into the minds of his military opponents, and he had, what all great commanders have not had, a sense of the reality of the civil population. He recommended himself to them by clemency and justice, and by holding his army under a strong hand ; they were willing therefore to help him, as far as they could, to his necessary supplies. Cities sent to submit themselves to him even when he seemed in most danger of defeat, and what the name of Rome itself had once meant to the tribes and nations was now engulfed in and identified with the name of Caesar. It was fitting therefore that—so soon now—he should fall nowhere but in Rome.

There remained one more necessary campaign. The East was quiet, Africa was quiet, Italy would be quiet as soon as he returned. Only in Spain, where the sons of Pompey had retreated, supported by Labienus, there was still revolt. After another brief visit to Rome he went there; he was absent from Italy for nine months, and once more he was victorious. Labienus and one Pompey were killed in battle. Only Sextus Pompey survived to carry on, at first, a guerilla warfare against Caesar's lieutenants, and—after Caesar's death to become a leader of pirates in the Mediterranean.

On the last visit to Rome Caesar had held a triumph, and honours had been showered on him by the Senate and the people. Now even those honours were outdone. Periods of thanksgiving were held; the titles of *Liberator* and *Imperator* were voted to him, and his descendants were to be *Imperator* also. A new temple —of Liberty—was to be raised. His person was declared sacrosanct. His chariot was to stand opposite the statue of the car of Jupiter; his image was to be borne in processions along with the images of the gods; statues were to be raised to him, and one especially was to be set up in the temple dedicated to Romulus, the fabled founder of Rome, and to bear the inscription *To the Unconquerable God*[1]. Deification had not previously existed in Rome. This newness and largeness of honour was accompanied by a similar offer of a newness and largeness of power. All magistracies were to be at his nomination, all magistrates under his dominion; he was to be at once consul and dictator; all the armies, all the finances, were to be at his absolute disposal; he was always to speak first in the Senate. Seventy-two lictors were to wait on him.

---

[1] Cf. Shakespeare: Julius Caesar I. ii. 115.
And this man
Is now become a god.

JULIUS CAESAR

He was the absolute lord of Rome and its world, but he was not to be called a king. The Republic, formally, was still a Republic, and the god Julius was no more than the first and best-deserving of its citizens.

Some hardly credible hope seems to have lingered in the minds of a few that he might indeed restore to Rome the actuality of a republican constitution. On one occasion, during the earlier visit, Cicero, who feared against hope, addressed him in the Senate:

'Though your achievements have embraced the whole State and the welfare of all its citizens, yet so far are you from setting the coping-stone on your greatest work that you have not yet laid the foundation which you design. . . . If, Caesar, this were to be the result of your immortal deeds, that after vanquishing your adversaries you should leave the commonwealth in the condition in which it now is, consider, I pray you, whether your superhuman prowess would not seem marvellous, indeed, but hardly glorious; for glory, I conceive, is the fame, spread throughout the world, of great services done to friends, to country, or to all mankind . . . you have still to recreate the Republic; you have still to enter on and to share with us, amidst all peace and quiet, the joy of your creation. Then, if you will, when you have paid to your country her due . . . it will be time to say that " you have lived long enough " . . . Among those who are yet to be born there will be controversy, as there has been among ourselves; some will extol your deeds, others perhaps will find something wanting, and that the one thing needful, unless you quench the flame of civil war by giving life to our State, so that men may ascribe the former to destiny, the latter to your design. Labour then for the verdict of that tribunal which will deliver judgement upon you many ages hence, a judgement perhaps more disinterested than ours; for posterity will judge without favour or partiality and, on the other hand, without rancour or jealousy.'

Caesar, on another occasion, remarked to his friends, when a certain prosecution was taking place, that everyone knew the facts, but ' what harm can it do to listen after this long time to a speech from Cicero ? ' Of that other speech the same thing might have been said. Almost everyone, except indeed a group of aristocrats, knew that it was impossible to recreate the Republic, for all the initiative depended on one man, and it is not so that republics can live, with whatever energy one man may arrange for them. But in fact Caesar never pretended or intended anything but himself, nor could the situation permit him any other possibility. It was he only who had achieved, as it seemed to him and to others, the salvation of the Roman world from its long agony of civil war and anarchy. It was he only who could continue to act. It was one of those moments in the history of Europe when all power of movement lay in one man. Yet that alone could not have formulated the new administration of what was to become Europe ; what decided that was the chance which gave it Augustus as a successor to Julius, and renewed the single power of initiative in government—a double need and a double genius to fill it.

Caesar, however, began the Reform. In what seems to us almost a symbol he established, among his earlier

JULIUS CAESAR

acts, the reform of the Calendar. The months were settled as they are to-day, and the name of July and the recurrence of the 29th February recall to us Julius discussing the solar year with the astronomers. He settled colonies and rebuilt cities—Carthage among them. He had measures prepared to help agricultural and industrial life. He proposed to drain marshes, to make roads, canals, harbours, to build temples, theatres, and above all libraries. He appointed a kind of Director of Education. He introduced laws to check the extravagance of the rich and to ease the distress of the poor. He equalized burdens, and invented methods to save the provinces from bad governors. He planned the census of the Roman world, by which a regular and proper administration of the whole might be made ; he proposed a just and effective Civil Service.

He did, and was, all that and more; but he was not a king. All the tradition of Rome since its earliest years was against that title. But rumours went about that he desired, or that others for him desired, that title also. He gave no signs. Once, as he rode into the city, someone from the crowd shouted the word at him ; he answered: ' I am not king but Caesar.' At a Roman festival Antony attempted to set a diadem on his head, as if from the Roman people. He refused, and ordered that the refusal should be noted in the public records. Yet the agitation concerning the possibility grew more intense. He wore a wreath of laurel, a red robe ; he had brought the Egyptian queen Cleopatra into the city, and visited her ; he had opened the Senate to the Gauls. These things rankled in some minds even more than the fact of his power. The possibility of his assassination had been uttered. He had dismissed his guard, after the Senate had sworn to protect him. His friends urged him to recall it; he answered that his life was of more value to his country than to himself; 'if I die, there will be civil war'; 'it is better to die than to live in fear of death.'

He was preparing to depart on new campaigns; this time to secure the frontiers of what was already, in effect, the Empire against eastern enemies without. One night at dinner, while he was signing letters, the guests were talking philosophically of what kind of death it was best to endure. Caesar flung a word: 'Sudden.' On the next day it was given him. The aristocratic conspirators had at last come to a plan—a plan which seems to have consisted merely in killing Caesar; after which, they seem vaguely to have supposed, everything would go right. They thought of killing Antony too, but Marcus Brutus, old Cato's son-in-law, on the highest principles dissuaded them. It was scrupulous but unintelligent.

On 15 March 44 B.C. the Dictator was carried in a litter to a meeting of the Senate in a hall outside Rome. His wife had implored him not to go, but some of the conspirators persuaded him not to disappoint the Senate. On his way a paper giving details of the plot was pushed at him. He took it but he had not read it when he came into the hall. He went to his own gilded chair and seated himself. A statue to Pompey stood close by. The conspirators came up around him. One of them spoke on behalf of his exiled brother; the rest, in a kind of pretended tumult of petition, laid hold on Caesar. He moved to rise. They caught down his

JULIUS CAESAR

toga ; one stabbed from behind. Caesar turned and seized the dagger. Then they were all on him ; they struck wildly, even wounding each other, but effectively. He felt his death upon him ; he dragged his toga round his head and fell. The bloody daggers were lifted up in triumph, between the dead Dictator and the Senate who were already in terrified flight.

The city shut its doors ; crowds filled the streets. The conspirators, calling on men to receive liberty, went through the streets, and at last, doubtful of the people, retreated to the Capitol. The body of Julius Caesar, 'liberator', 'father of his country', 'imperator', 'unconquerable god', was carried by his slaves to his house. The moans and tears of the crowd accompanied it, to mingle with the tears and shrieks of his wife.

In his own house Mark Antony shut himself up, with the private treasure and private papers of Caesar, and waited his opportunity. The night of 15 March 44 B.C. fell upon the city and the world.

CHARLEMAGNE

THE name of Charlemagne, from whom in effect the second Roman Empire begins, differs in one respect from the name of Caesar. The tales and traditions about Caesar concentrate on him as a figure of history. But Charlemagne is both a figure of history and a figure of myth. We know much less about him than we do about Caesar. But the fancies and inventions about him are thicker, and when literature remembers him it often does so as a fantastic ruler of more than mortal stature, who still sits somewhere in the heart of a mountain waiting his hour to return and save the world.

Yet that thorn-bearded figure, who conversed with angels in dreams, and whose lance carried the head of the Roman spear which had pierced the side of Christ, whose sword was called Joyeuse and whose ring had magical properties, is not the greatest heroic figure even in his own Court. One of his own lords, if less of a ruler, was a greater fighter, and the last stand of Roland is known where Charlemagne is only a name. A small ambush in the mountains when the mounted rearguard of the Frank king's retreating force was destroyed by the native mountaineers has become the tale of the great stand of the peers of France against multitudinous foes, and the horn of Roncesvalles which Charlemagne heard three days' journey away has sounded for twelve centuries to the imagination of Europe.

CHARLEMAGNE

Yet myth and history derive from the same fact. Round about the year A.D. 800, in a long period of history which is only now beginning to be cleared for us, among moving peoples and falling and rising kingdoms, among warring religions and rushes of old and new creeds, there rises a moment of stability and order, of culture and belief. In that moment the hands of the Pope set on the head of its military champion, named Charles and called ' the Great ', a crown which is called Roman, and the Pope's voice renews for him the old Roman title *Imperator*. He is to be, however greatly changed the time, what Caesar was; he is to order the world and to bring peace and justice to men. Then he dies, and the darkness flows back, and the tumults return, and two hundred years go by before the abbeys and the universities begin to be built, and Europe again begins. But when it does the name of Charlemagne, the title of Emperor, and the idea of government re-emerge blessed by that great moment's vision in the past.

What then was the man of so high a moment ? He came in a period between two great civilizations, the Imperial Rome which was past and the medieval Europe which was to be. The profoundest difference between those two civilizations is that one was based on the person of the Emperor, the other on a metaphysical idea. The Roman administration, the civil service of the Emperor, had broken down everywhere, except in the districts round Byzantium (now Constantinople) to which the capital of the empire had in A.D. 330 been moved. Rome itself was left to its lay magistrates and to its Bishop. That name Bishop signifies the new

STORIES OF GREAT NAMES

universal administration of the new Thing which had entered Europe from the Near East—the Christian idea, the Church which expressed and embodied that idea on earth, and the orders of priesthood, of which the Bishop was the highest,[1] who managed and directed the whole Church. Each bishop was the head of a diocese, and those dioceses were now extended over the whole of what had been the Roman Empire and far beyond it. To be in obedience to that complex administration was to be in agreement with a particular set of ideas about life and (more or less) to adopt a particular way of life. To be against those ideas and that life was to be hostile to the administration which enforced them.

The bishops, however, were primarily administrators of the Church; next, of civic life; and only, thirdly, and in cases of urgent necessity, of military. The old territory of the empire was occupied and disputed by the armed forces of a hundred tribes and peoples. The Franks were in Gaul, the Lombards in Italy. Some were more destructive than others of what remained of Roman culture. Some were obedient, some hostile, to what was stable in the new Christendom. It still seemed possible that Europe, in spite of all efforts by the bishops, by the remote successors of Julius Caesar at Byzantium, by this captain or that general, might go down into savagery. There was still industry, commerce, learning, piety, art, but the danger of complete collapse was over and under all. The whole of the old Empire in the west was in as perilous a state as Rome

---

[1] The hierarchy of the Church contained other officers—archbishops, patriarchs, cardinals. But there is no higher sacramental power than the episcopal, except in so far as it may be claimed for the Pope who is the Bishop of Rome.

CHARLEMAGNE

itself had been when the greatest child of the Julian house opened his eyes in 102 B.C.

In, or about, the year A.D. 744, Charles, called the Great, was born, probably in Gaul, then the land of the Franks, but not yet France. His first appearance in history is when he was twelve years old. In the cold and snow of a Gallic winter there came from Italy the chief bishop of the west, the bishop of Rome, the Pope Stephen II, taking that anxious and difficult journey to ask for help. Italy had been invaded and Rome was threatened by the Lombards, a people originally from central Europe by the Elbe. They had but lately accepted the Christian idea in its fullness, and they were still regarded by the Romans as typical pagan barbarians. What power the Byzantine Emperor still had in South Italy was hardly sufficient to protect itself, and quite insufficient to defend Rome. Yet if Rome was finally subjected to the Lombards, its independence and its prestige, almost its power, would be lost.

In Gaul was the father of Charles, Pepin the Frank, a Christian and a friend of the Roman bishopric. It was to him that the Pope fled as a suppliant, and to meet the Pope came the young boy, Pepin's son. In that first uncertain picture Charles salutes Stephen, and the great alliance is prophesied. Pepin accepted the Pope's request, defeated the Lombards, took from them twenty-one cities, and bestowed all his seizures upon the Pope; then he withdrew again across the Alps.

Thus, when twelve years later, Charlemagne succeeded his father as King of the Franks, his eyes were already directed towards Italy and Rome. His mind had been so formed as to accept easily the idea that he should be the military protector of the greatest of the bishoprics. He believed firmly in the Christian doctrine; he was prepared to regard himself as the champion of Christian doctrine. But also, partly from that cause, he desired to establish stability, a stability which, as he saw it, had three chief elements—a strong military power to overcome other threatening peoples, a strong religious power to direct souls to God, and as strong an intellectual power as could be created that men might use to God's glory the minds God had given them. All his activities had these three things for their purpose.

The first of these three things occupied him almost every year of his life. In each spring he would summon together his army to some chosen place. Theoretically all his male subjects owed him military service; practically he compounded for a strong, willing, and well-armed proportion. He saw to it that his army was an army, and not a horde; he made it therefore a thing to be used effectively at the will of its commander. He ordered his underlords to send their men with arms and equipment, with wagons containing spades, axes, and other instruments, with rations for three months, and proper clothing. The levies were to keep together, to do no harm to the population, and to be at the appointed place by the appointed time. All the levies having come in, he moved against whatever enemy seemed the most threatening—against Saxons in the north-east, Lombards in Italy, Saracens in Spain.

CHARLEMAGNE

Against these and other enemies, such as the Avars in remote Hungary or the pirates from the north, Charlemagne all his life had to conduct campaigns or establish guardhouses. The spring expedition moved out year after year, and the fame of the terrible King of the Franks spread all over Europe. There is a story of how, when he came down into Italy, Desiderius, King of the Lombards, stood on a high tower of Pavia with an exiled Frankish noble Othar. From there they saw the advance of the army, and as the mass of the vanguard came into sight Desiderius asked: 'Is Charlemagne among these?' and Othar answered: 'No.' The king said in great distress: 'But what shall we do if greater forces come with him?' Othar answered: 'When he comes you will not mistake him, but I cannot guess what will happen to us then.' There appeared then all the household of Charlemagne, the paladins and peers, and the king said: 'There he must be'—Othar said: 'No.' And then came the bishops and priests of the Chapel, abbots and cross-bearers and thurifers, and the king began to sob and say: 'Let us hide ourselves in the earth.' But Othar, himself shaking with fear, answered: 'When all the fields bear a harvest of iron, when rivers of iron pour against the city, you will know that Charlemagne is near.' And as he spoke the whole day darkened with a black cloud moving from the west, and out of the cloud came flashings and lightnings of steel; and the cloud resolved itself into an immense host of men marching all in iron armour, and all the open earth was covered with that iron movement. In the midst of it appeared Charlemagne himself, clad in iron, carrying an iron spear in his left hand, his right lying always on his iron sword, an iron shield slung about him, and his very horse of the colour of iron. All this vision of iron was less than the iron hearts of Charlemagne and his men. The walls of the city shook and the inhabitants trembled. The king gazed in terror, when Othar, turning on him and crying out ' This is the man you so desired to see '

fell as one dead at Desiderio's feet.

The story was written down within a hundred years of the reign of Charlemagne; so greatly had he impressed his world. The defeated Lombards were compelled to yield cities to the Pope; the defeated Saxons to give up cannibalism and sorcery and human sacrifices, and to accept the Christian faith. Gradually all their districts passed under the supreme sovereignty of Charles, and were, as much as any land then was, in order and at peace.

But of all these military operations, that which is best known is the tale of Roncesvalles; the tale which was so well known within fifty years after Charlemagne's death that the clerks would not trouble to write it, that the Norman minstrel sang before the battle of Hastings, that has been translated and again translated in our own day as poetry and not as history, that has given a common proverb to English colloquialism[1] and common allusions to English poetic tradition. It was a fact which became a myth, but the fact did not very much matter, and the myth has mattered very much indeed.

[1] A Roland for an Oliver.

CHARLEMAGNE

Spain had been part of the Empire which Caesar founded and Augustus ordered. In the days of Charlemagne, however, it was no longer a part of Christendom, nor did it fully become so for another seven hundred years. But neither was it a dim chaotic land where wandering peoples clashed together or the servants of the Pope or the Byzantine Emperor maintained a difficult loyalty. Something quite different had happened; another religion, another culture, had seized it. The Prophet Mahomet had died in A.D. 632; the great creed which is called either by his name or by the simple title of Islam had seized Egypt by 642, by 670 had reached Tunis, and had subjugated all North Africa soon after 700. In 711 the first attack on Spain was launched, and the peninsula was occupied and the attack carried over into France by 732. Thence, however, it receded, but all middle and south Spain acknowledged the suzerainty of the Sultan of Damascus. A civilization was soon to exist there by which the struggling culture of Europe was a poor thing, and the idea of Islam lay contiguous to the Christian kingdoms in the west as it threatened Byzantium in the east. It would not capture Byzantium till 1453; it did not completely lose Spain till a little later.

Charlemagne never seriously contested Spain; he had enough to do without provoking another war. But he was anxious to maintain a border district to protect his frontiers, and in 778, at the invitation of an Arab governor of Barcelona, he crossed the Pyrenees on what turned out to be no more than an unsuccessful raid. Even so, it was rather political than religious,

STORIES OF GREAT NAMES

since he was called in by a Mahommedan chieftain, began the war by seizing the Christian city of Pampeluna, and was attacked by a Christian mountain people called Basques. He went as far as Saragossa, which he did not take, and the army, having cleared the southern borders of the Pyrenees, began its return across them. The rearguard, commanded by a certain Roland, Count of the Marches, was overwhelmed in an ambush by the Basques and completely destroyed.

As such things do, however—at least, sometimes—the facts were translated into a quite different tale. The comparatively few Basques were turned into multitudinous armies of Saracens. The commander of the rearguard was turned into the Twelve Paladins of France. The confused destruction of his force became the heroic resistance of those great champions to their Islamic enemies, and their eventual death upon heaps of their foes became a more sublime spectacle than any victory. Before death had claimed them, while Roland and his brother Oliver and the Archbishop Turpin were still alive, Roland sounded his horn thrice, which he had refused to do at the beginning of the attack, and far away Charlemagne heard it, and was twice persuaded, by the false Lord Ganelon who had betrayed the Paladins to their foes, that he was mistaken. But the third time he knew it and returned with all his host, and when they had again reached the pass of Roncesvalles they found the bodies of the Paladins lying, and that of Roland, who had died last of all, with his face turned towards Spain, ' that Charles and all the army might see he died as a gallant liegeman, looking towards the enemy. . . . Count Roland is dead, and his soul

CHARLEMAGNE

is gone to the paradise of God.' Then the king took great vengeance for his servants—the sun stood still while his host was slaying—and as for Ganelon he had him torn to pieces by wild horses as a just punishment. For Ganelon in romance is one of that band of immortal traitors, among whom are Judas who betrayed Christ and Mordred who betrayed King Arthur, and others of the same evil kind. Such was the basis, and such the creation, of the *Song of Roland*.

This is at least an example of the way in which the myth of Charlemagne grew, in an age when written records were rare and printed records did not exist. It will not do, however, as is too often a modern habit, to underrate some facts because others have been turned into fable. The great war between Charlemagne and the Saracens is a high invention of poetry. The Coronation of Charles is a mere fact. Yet the Coronation is hardly inferior to the poem in its effect upon European history and European imagination. It is the first great sign that that great world of Rome was capable of recreating itself and was not to go down utterly into oblivion like many another empire of the past. It has been said justly that Europe ought to have died. But she did not.

When the Lombards and the Saxons had been subdued, and peoples beyond them, there were four powers to be reckoned with, or rather four who had to reckon with each other. There was Islam, but the Spanish borderland lay between Charlemagne and Islam; there was Charlemagne himself; there was the Pope as the head of the network of dioceses and bishops in the west; there was the Emperor at Byzantium. Our histories often call him the Eastern Emperor because of his geographical position and the earlier division of the Roman Empire into east and west. But in fact he was not so regarded. The tradition of Julius still lived, and the Byzantine throne held, at least in theory, the ruler of the whole world. Only the power of that ruler was negligible in the west. He could do nothing to protect Christendom; his hands were full with his own enemies in the east. He claimed obedience still, but less and less was any commander or bishop disposed to yield it. The Pope had other reasons for not acknowledging the imperial suzerainty. For the Pope, more than any other single person, was the symbol of that universal and philosophical idea which had substituted itself for the old Roman idea. Every bishop, every priest, regarded himself as being subject to the civil authority only in certain respects; no bishop and no priest would admit that the office he held in the Church could be subordinated to a secular head. The Pope, least of all, could admit it. He was the sign of a thing more important than all civil government, however exalted; he was the sign of the Christian Faith and the Catholic Church which expressed that Faith.

Yet the Faith lives in the world, and has to do with men in their daily relations. It was not the business of the Pope to govern Europe in civil things, nor to defend by arms the safety of the Church he administered. Some governor and defender, however, there must be, and the thought of that age, still under the influence of Julius and eight hundred years' tradition of universal authority, still dreamed of an Emperor. There had,

CHARLEMAGNE

in the past, been an Emperor of the East and an Emperor of the West. There was now an ineffectual Emperor *in* the East ; might there not be . . . ?

We do not know whose mind first bridged the space between the old dream and the present reality. It may have been the Pope's ; it may, more likely, have been some now unremembered servant or diplomat of the Pope's. It may, less probably, have been Charlemagne or one of Charlemagne's servants. It was certainly the Pope who consented to carry the thought into act, and re-establish in the west a title which was to last for more than a thousand years, until it was abolished in favour of Napoleon's title of Emperor of the French in 1804. It was Napoleon who spoke of ' Our predecessor Charlemagne ', and though all imperial titles in the west have vanished since his time, yet it would be rash to say that the thing itself is either dead or is supposed to be dead. It has helped to save Europe twice in the past ; it may help to consolidate her again.

It was the year 800. Charlemagne, then a man of about fifty-six, had come down into Italy, and was keeping Christmas in Rome. He was then a tall man—almost seven feet, it was reported. ' Of a large and strong body,' says a contemporary description, ' a round head, large and piercing eyes, a rather large nose, and a cheerful and alert countenance. He had a firm step and a princely bearing, a clear but not very strong voice.' He was good at all physical exercises—especially riding and swimming. He had, like his predecessor Julius, an active and curious mind. He had also, unlike his predecessor Julius, a great sense of personal religion; he was a devout Christian, and took an interest in the theology of his religion. Theology had come in with Christianity so strongly as to be almost a popular subject; the nature of Christ and the means of redemption were discussed in the streets as well as the schools wherever the old Roman culture still endured, and the civil rulers of Europe presided or at least were present when the bishops of the Church met in council to determine what was the true Faith—' held by all, at all times, and in all places '—on any disputed point of doctrine. Charlemagne had a peculiar interest in such matters, besides a strong personal piety. It was these things also which suited the new office to which, willingly or unwillingly, he was to be called.

He said afterwards that he was unaware of what was intended; it may have been so. What happened was expressed in a single act, as significant as the first step which the first legionary of Caesar's took across the Rubicon. It was Christmas Day in the year 800. In the great church of St. Peter's at Rome the Pope was saying Mass. On all sides of the candle-lit altar gold and gems flashed back the light of the multitudinous other candles that lit the church. Immediately before and below the altar was the subterranean cave where, it was said, lay the body of St. Peter, from whom the Popes claimed to hold authority: a little farther away knelt the King of the Franks, dressed out of courtesy in the Roman manner and not in that of his own people. Beyond and around him were the rest of the congregation, ecclesiastics of all ranks, officers and populace of Rome, dukes and counts and captains of Charles's

CHARLEMAGNE

household and army, chiefs and lords of allied peoples. ' Assuredly if he himself was ignorant of what was about to happen neither the Roman citizens nor the Frankish courtiers shared his ignorance. There was a hush of expectation throughout the dim basilica, and all eyes were directed towards the kneeling figure in Roman garb at the tomb of the Apostle.'[1]

The sacred ceremony drew to its end. The Pope sang the last phrase of the Rite. The moment of private devotions succeeded, and Charles still knelt in prayer. As he was about to rise he saw the Pope descending towards him, and he hesitated. The Pope came up, holding in his hands a golden crown; he set it on the King's head; he cried out, and all the great congregation shouted with him: ' Life and victory to Charles Augustus, crowned by God's will, the mighty and pacific Emperor.'

The word had been formally uttered; the deed had been spectacularly done. The Pope, following ancient custom, prostrated himself at the feet of the Emperor; the church rang with acclamation. From the building, already five centuries old, into which on that Christmas morning the King of the Franks had come, the Emperor, solemnly recognized and crowned, passed out. Christendom in the West had again an accepted secular head. Charles altered his own style to correspond. He was no longer a mere chieftain, of however great a people; he held now, in some sense, a sacred office. It was new, for never before had an Emperor been crowned in Rome, and certainly never before had the coronation been so solemnly religious or the priestly

[1] Hodgkin. *Italy and her Invaders.* Vol. VIII.

STORIES OF GREAT NAMES

authority in the Church bestowed the Crown. Yet, though so sanctified, it was very old. 'Charles,' wrote the Emperor in his dispatches, 'crowned by the will of God, Roman Emperor, Augustus ... in the year of our consulship 1.' He was not only a new Emperor; he was the old magistrate. There was issued from his capital of Aachen (or Aix) an oath to be taken by all his subjects: 'I order that every man in my whole kingdom, whether ecclesiastic or layman, each one according to his prayer and his purpose, who may have before promised fidelity to me in the king's name, shall now repeat that promise to me in my name as Caesar. And those who may not yet have made that promise shall now all do so, from twelve years old and upwards. And let this be done in public, so that all may understand how many and how great things are contained in that oath, not merely, as many have hitherto supposed, that they shall not conspire against the Emperor's life, nor let his enemies into the realm, nor be privy to any treachery against him. Far greater duties than these are involved in this oath.' The oath then enforces the obligation of each man to abide in the service of God and to dedicate to Him all his bodily and intellectual powers; to abstain from perjury and fraud of all kinds; not to filch the lands of the Emperor nor conceal his fugitive slaves; neither by force nor fraud to do any injury to the holy churches of God, to orphans, widows or strangers, 'forasmuch as our Lord the Emperor, under God and His saints, has been appointed protector and defender of all such'; not to lay waste the land which a man holds in fief from the king in order to enrich his own adjoining property;

CHARLEMAGNE

always to follow the king's banner to war; not to hinder the execution of his writ, nor to strive to pervert the course of justice in the provincial assembly.

There were, of course, great difficulties with the established Imperial power still ruling in Byzantium. At the moment of Charles's coronation the throne was occupied by a woman, the Empress Irene. Charles sent ambassadors to soothe the shocked anger which the eastern court might feel at his assumption of the unique title, and to propose his own political marriage to the Empress. The proposal came to nothing, for in the year 802 she was deposed, and the two thrones remained unfriendly for some eight years. At the end of that time relations were established, and in 812 at Aachen the ambassadors of the Byzantine Emperor acknowledged the imperial title and authority of Charles. It was the definition of the political idea of Europe for six hundred years, until the fall of Byzantium before the Turks in 1453.

There was yet another empire and mighty ruler with whom, though only from a distance and by rare embassies, Charlemagne established relations. Away at Bagdad lived, at that time, one whose name has been almost more familiar to English readers than that of Charlemagne himself, the magnificent and famous Caliph, Haroun-al-Raschid. High courtesies were exchanged, and presents; in the great parks around the palace at Aix there dwelt for some eight years an elephant whose arrival in Western Europe suggested the wonders of that great and almost mythical culture which lay in lands beyond the sun-rising where, on cushions of state in slim-pillared palaces, among his own diplomats, sages and poets, the Commander of the Faithful listened to equally strange tales of the gigantic and long-bearded figure on whose head among the farthest rocks and seas had rested the latest crown of Rome.

Nor indeed was it only in military force, or by awful and sacred office that Charlemagne was a worthy rival of Haroun's. He had another claim. He regarded religion as more important than intellect, but he was not one of those fierce bigots who disparage the intellect, and all his life he did what he could to create and maintain schools and homes of culture among the uncertain warfare of the west. His court in its day was, on a much lower level, like the court of the Caliph Haroun at Bagdad, a centre of civilization and learning. But what was easy for Haroun was difficult for Charlemagne who had come to his throne after so much of the Roman culture had been destroyed. He invited all the learned men of whom he could hear to Aix. This was his favourite city; here he built a palace and a great church, with pillars, marbles, candelabra, and brass gates brought from cities of Italy. In Aix he was able to lead his own private life, so far as his wars and policies left him any. He was himself by no means poorly educated for that time. He had a good vocabulary; he could speak 'almost too fluently'. He understood Latin and Greek; he began to make up a grammar of the Frankish language. He is said to have kept a kind of anthology of old songs and ballads, and to have known them by heart, and he even composed Frankish names for the twelve months as if to displace the old Roman names. July, for example, was to be

CHARLEMAGNE

Heivimanoth, or Hay-month; October, Stormmonth; December, Holy-month, because of Christmas; January, Winter-month; May, Love-month. He tried to combine, as it were, the traditions of his native land with the other tradition of Rome; he began that idea of a local loyalty and of a universal loyalty which has been for so long the dream of Europe.

The chief man of learning at his court was named Alcuin. In 781 Charlemagne had arrived at Pavia in Italy where there was presented to him a man from Yorkshire, one of the northern counties of England, who had been sent to Rome on business connected with the diocese of York. The two seem to have become immediate friends. They were both Northerners, both devout; both loved culture and learning. Alcuin, when young, had come especially under the great influence of the Roman poet Virgil, whose greatest work, the *Aeneid*, had been composed in honour of Augustus and the peace he had brought to the Roman world. And though in later life Alcuin preferred the Latin of the theologians and devotional writers, yet he never lost that passion for the classic writers. He was invited by Charles to return with him to Aix, and this, having obtained permission from his bishop, he did.

At Aix he organized the Palace School. Such schools at most courts were for the sons of kings or great lords, but Charlemagne treated study too seriously to limit it in such a manner. The school was opened to other promising students, and there remains a story of how Charlemagne, having examined the work of the boys, addressed them, ' rather like thunder than speech ', praising the boys of lower birth and severely rebuking those of higher. He was perhaps hardly fair, because by definition the boys of lower families were precisely those of exceptional ability, whereas the others were there because of their birth and not because of their capacity. On such a subject one can but say that he meant well, and that the declarations of so great a monarch gave an exceptional stimulus to the work of the young scholars.

The school, however, was not Alcuin's only business. He had to order and encourage all court learning. He was the equivalent of a modern Minister of Education, although the education was by no means for all. He was the king's adviser also in Church matters and in political to the extent that he helped to lay down the principles of what was almost the first medieval government. His correspondence with Charles still remains—letters exchanged freely between two friends, two able men, two leaders of what for a little while it seemed might become a stable and widespread civilization. Around them the busy intellectual life went on; manuscripts were copied, music was practised, languages studied, and, as if in a symbol, one of the sciences in which Charles himself took a keen interest was astronomy, and the searching out of the starry lamps of heaven.

So the great Emperor ruled, and it is little wonder that his name grew into a myth. His authority, as councillor if not as overlord, was felt in the Saxon kingdoms of Britain; he concluded a peace with the Danes; he held Gaul and Germany and guarded the Pyrenees; he was the friend and champion of the Pope, and ruled North Italy; he was saluted as

CHARLEMAGNE

Emperor by the Emperor in Byzantium ; he received the courtesies of the Caliph Haroun from far in the East. He supported and defended the creed of Christendom, and the orthodox belief rooted and spread itself under his care. He attempted again to recover the ' sweetness and light ' of knowledge and humane learning. For a few years he held the western world still.

It did not last. In the year 814, when he was about seventy years old, he was attacked by fever and pleurisy. He lay dying, and already the empire that he had made was shaking under his relaxing hand. He had but one son left, whom he had himself crowned as his successor. But that son had not his father's energy or genius, and was known not to have it. The empire was threatened from without by great fleets, the Northmen coming down the coasts and up the rivers from Scandinavia, the Saracens raiding the Mediterranean islands and the Italian shores.

It was 28 January 814 when the Emperor died. He was buried at Aix, and over his tomb they carved his epitaph.

' Under this tombstone is laid the body of Charles, the great and orthodox Emperor, who gloriously enlarged the kingdom of the Franks, and prosperously governed it for forty-seven years. He died a septuagenarian in the year of our Lord 814.'

But as the Empire broke up after his death, and a medley of war and uncertainty passed over Europe for another two hundred years, the myth of Charlemagne grew greater and the place of his burial was changed. It was said that he had not truly died ; he had seemed

STORIES OF GREAT NAMES

to die, but in fact he had been carried to a great cavern deep in some Saxon mountain, and there, surrounded by his paladins, he sits on his throne, crowned, sceptred, armed, with the book of the Gospels on his knees, till the day comes upon which he shall ride out again to bring victory, peace, and justice to the agonized peoples of the west.

JOAN OF ARC

As Charlemagne is a myth of the founders of the Middle Ages, so Joan of Arc is a name of their last period. Between them lay a great civilization—an immense world of action, of art, philosophy. That world, as was said before, was a world which differed profoundly from the Europe which had preceded it, for its base was metaphysical, and the centre of that base was a dogma or rather a group of dogmas which composed the Christian Faith. Much went on in the Middle Ages which was utterly opposed to the morals of the Faith. But this did not alter the fact that all the activities of that time were expressed in terms of a common religion as they had not been before and have hardly been since. They held a common religion and they had general ideas of a common union. Under many and profound differences they felt themselves to be *one*.

That unity, merely imagined or hoped as it might be, began at last to break down. There were many causes for the failure. It is a failure which we are in part attempting to redeem to-day by the efforts of the League of Nations. The last gathering in Europe to which came the leaders of thought and action was the Council of Constance. Between the Council of Constance, held 1414-18, and the first meeting of the League at Geneva, no similar gathering was known. There were meetings of statesmen or monarchs, after war or to avoid war. There was no attempt to gather

STORIES OF GREAT NAMES

Europe together and provide it with a newly effective organization of life.

Since this book is not a history but only an account of certain great and moving names, there is no need to discuss in detail the causes of the break-down, which in practice meant the break-up, of the Middle Ages. Both terms apply to the one cause which it is necessary to mention here : the Rise of the Nations. The weakening of the idea of a unity led to an increase in the prestige of the parts of that unity—England, France, Spain, the principalities of Italy and Germany ; and this increase meant the break-up of the whole into those parts. Nationality triumphed, and one of the great champions of nationality, though she would not have called it that, was Joan of Arc.

She would not have called it that, and she would have been horrified to learn the extremes to which it went. She certainly had no idea of the Nations breaking away from whatever unity in Christendom they could achieve. She desired greatly that they should live in brotherhood together, and make a common cause. But nevertheless, not by her will, she helped the rise of the Nations in her own day ; and since her day her patriotism has been remembered and her internationalism forgotten. Her name has done more than she thought or wanted. She became a saint to Europe, and a myth to literature. She, Julius Caesar, and Cleopatra alone unite the persons of Shakespeare's plays with the persons of Bernard Shaw's, and what better proof of mythology could be given ?

It was the year 1412. Henry IV was on the English

JOAN OF ARC

throne, with two more years to reign; his son, Henry V, a great general, was to succeed him. The wars between England and France, conducted always in France, for no force crossed the sea to invade England, and it was France which the Kings of England claimed, had already been raging since 1338. It is not quite correct to call them England and France for we attribute to them our present ideas of those names, whereas it is precisely to Joan of Arc that we owe, at least in part, even those present ideas. The feudal lord of England was at war, for an intricate legal claim, with the feudal lord of France. France, during the fifty years before Joan's birth, had been swept by plague—the Black Death—as, for that matter, had England. But also she had been swept by English armies, and betrayed by her own. When Joan was six a treaty was come to, by which the Crown of France, after the death of its then possessor, was to pass to Henry V of England. The French king's heir, called the Dauphin of France, was thus disinherited.

But in 1420 Henry V died. On behalf of the baby Henry VI, his uncle the Duke of Bedford, ruled in France. He occupied Paris and all the strong fortresses of the north except Orleans, and that he was besieging. A great many of the French feudal lords acknowledged the English claim. The Dauphin, the French king also having died, maintained a poor resistance, in the southern half of the country.

On the eastern side of France was a district known as Lorraine, dangerously situated between France and the dominions of the Emperor—the localized monarchy of what had once been intended to be a universal lordship.

STORIES OF GREAT NAMES

Domremy was a village of Lorraine, and in Domremy Joan was born—it is said in 1412, upon the feast of the Epiphany, that is, of the adoration of the infant Christ by the wise men of the East. Her father and mother were of low social rank, but landowners, of course, as most of the medieval country folk were, holding their own legal rights of pasture in common with their village neighbours, and of some standing themselves in the village. The district had not suffered directly from the English invasions, but it had been raided by the troop of the Duke of Burgundy, a French lord allied to the English, and Domremy once burnt. The effects of the general wars between the great lords had come to it. Nevertheless there was no particular reason to expect any man of Lorraine who was not compelled to follow his lord to take part in the struggle, though in general the feeling of the village seems to have been strongly in favour of the Dauphin. The children used to fight, on behalf of France, the children of the Burgundian village of Maney near by.

Joan was brought up in the usual way to be of use in the house and the fields. Her father was a good but firm man; he stood no nonsense from his children. Joan said he kept her in much subjection. She learned the creed and attended the services of the Church; other learning she had none. It was no doubt a healthy but certainly a hard life, though there were times of holiday and festivity. There was, near the village, a beech tree, called the Ladies' Tree or the Fairies' Tree. Legend declared that in old days the lord of the place, Pierre Granier, had met under it or its predecessor a Fairy Lady, as in another legend

JOAN OF ARC

Thomas the Rhymer was said to have met in the woodland the Queen of Fairyland. Granier's family still ruled in the district, and the then lord and his wife would sometimes walk under the tree with their daughters. The young people of the village held dances by it; about it and about a well called the 'Well of the Thorn', tales were told and half-believed rites practised. On a particular Sunday in the spring of each year the boys and girls were accustomed to go there; they ate and played under the Tree and afterwards drank of the Well. Also they took nuts as offerings to the Tree and the Well. It was the tradition of the place, its amusement, and its joyous romantic thrill.

But though Joan went with the rest to the Tree it was to the other centre, the village church, that she paid more devotion. Years afterwards those who had grown up with her recalled her piety. If their accounts were all that remained of her life, we might suspect her of a certain priggishness; there is a tale of her rebuking the Sacristan for not ringing the bell for Mass, and promising him gifts of wool if he did his duty properly. This must have been when she was older, but many of his companions told how she would not play with them as often as they wished. 'I and my friends told her she was too religious.' 'We made fun of her.' It seems probable that Joan could hold her own; she was a girl of strong words and action. There was one Burgundian in Domremy: 'I should have been quite willing for them to cut off his head—always had it pleased God,' she said of him later. She nursed a friend when he was ill; she was a good worker, spinning

STORIES OF GREAT NAMES

and taking her turn in looking after her father's sheep or pigs. 'I fear no woman in Rouen for spinning and sewing,' she said at her trial. She worked always for her own family; there was no need of hiring her out to other villagers.

She was thirteen—that is, it was about the year 1425—when the great opening of her vocation took place. It was a day in summer, and about noon she was in the garden of her father's house. She was alone; it seemed to her that there was a great light by her right side, and that a voice spoke to her. 'I was very much frightened,' she said simply. This was the beginning of what are called her Voices, the beginning also of the salvation of France, and of the triumph of the idea of nationalism in the mind of Europe.[1]

The light and the Voice recurred at other times. At first she had only felt them as something which ought to be reverenced. But by the third occasion she thought it was the Voice of an angel, one of those high and marvellous spiritual beings who, in the theology of her Church, are understood to be part of the joyous heavenly creation. She came to understand that the Voice which spoke to her came from one of the greatest of these beings, St. Michael, who is called the prince of the heavenly host. It said to her: 'It is necessary that you go to France.' On her own witness it spoke to her two or three times a week, and presently it told her that other powers would come to her—St. Margaret

---

[1] This is not the place to discuss the nature of the Voices; the Church holds them, as Joan did, to be supernatural. There are, of course, other opinions; a necessary condition of any opinion is to remember that Joan was physically one of the healthiest girls who have ever lived.

JOAN OF ARC

and St. Catherine, who are not angels but the spirits of Christian martyrs in the years of persecution. She had now begun to live two lives, her ordinary friendly life in cottage and country, and this secret life of attention, instruction, and discipleship. She had to be habituated to the idea of her mission; Joan was not one of those who believe easily that they are chosen by God to save the world. It was her sense of obedience and not of her own glory which eventually moved her. Her Voices began to move her to action. They said: 'Go to France'; 'Go, raise the siege of Orleans'. 'Go to Vaucouleurs.'

Vaucouleurs was a castled place some distance off, governed for the Dauphin by an officer called Robert de Baudricourt. It became more and more clear to Joan that the heavenly beings who were speaking to her were assuring her that it was the will of God that France should be redeemed by her means. She dedicated herself to obedience and to the mission. There was the question of telling her parents, but she determined to say nothing before she left. Her father was a good man but he was not likely to believe either that the heavenly beings were directing his daughter or that they were directing her to run the very great risks which a journey to the headquarters of the Dauphin would involve. He would be likely to take firm steps to keep her still ' in subjection '.

Not to her parents but to another she dropped one phrase; meeting the single village champion of Burgundy one day she called to him : ' Friend, if you were not a Burgundian I would tell you something.' He thought it was mere chaff, and that she was referring to some possibility of her marriage. It was chaff, no doubt, but of a more celestial kind.

It was 1428, and she was about sixteen. At last she had recourse to a cousin, a married man, living in a village a couple of miles from Vaucouleurs. His wife was ill and Joan managed to be asked to go and look after her. It was permitted; she stayed with her relations and convinced them sufficiently to persuade her cousin to take her to Vaucouleurs. A first visit took place in May 1428; it had no result. Robert de Baudricourt, either then or at the beginning of the next visit, told her cousin to box her ears and send her home to her father. She returned certainly to Domremy, but in February 1429 she was back at the castle. De Baudricourt hesitated still, but presently he found himself compelled to take notice. Rumours of her and her mission had begun to get abroad; it was known what reason she had given for her journey to Vaucouleurs. The curious watched for her; a young priest studied her as she knelt privately in prayer before the altar in the crypt of the church, which is still to be seen. Prophetesses and wandering workers of miracles —or at any rate those who claimed to work miracles— were no uncommon thing in the Middle Ages. They were frowned on by the Church authorities, and harried by the secular, but they wandered about, performing more or less authentic cures on sick persons and making what living they could. The Duke of Lorraine, who was in bad health, heard of the Lorraine girl who was talking of her mission and sent for her. When she arrived he began to ask questions about his illness. She answered that she must go to France. He tried to

JOAN OF ARC

keep the conversation on himself, but it would not do. She would not talk at all of him and very little of herself; only that she would pray to God for his health, and he was to give her men, and send his son, and have her taken to France. What he did do was to send her back to Vaucouleurs. He could not know, but it was unfortunate for his future fame.

There, however, in her first stay she had made some friends, Jean de Metz, a knight, among them. He had seen her, in a worn red dress, and spoken to her, and, as now was so often to happen in the months ahead, the strong spirit of the strong country girl impressed and dominated him. She seems to have been tall, well-formed, good to look on, with a frank and joyous face, crowned with short black hair. He asked her what her business there was. She said that de Baudricourt did not believe and would not help her, but she must get to the King, even if she had to wear down her legs doing it; nobody could help France—no one—but she, though she would rather be at home, but she must do it because it was her lord's will. 'Who then is your lord?' he asked, as if speaking of a feudal superior. She answered: 'My lord is God.' He was so moved that, as if in feudal homage, he touched her hand in pledge of loyalty and swore 'to be her man'. He offered to escort her: when did she want to start? 'Sooner to-day than to-morrow, and sooner to-morrow than afterwards,' she answered. The visit to the Duke caused the start to be postponed. When she returned, however, things went more quickly. De Baudricourt consented and gave her a safe conduct. A little group of six men went with her—two gentlemen, Jean de Metz

STORIES OF GREAT NAMES

and Bertrand de Poulengey; two of the King's people —one of his Messengers and one of his Archers; and two horsemen of Jean's. She wore, for convenience and safety, a man's dress, and the seven riders made what haste they could towards the tall ancient castle of Chinon, where the Dauphin then was. For fear of the bands of Burgundians and presently of the English, they travelled chiefly by night and rested by day. Whenever they could they heard Mass, but it could only be done twice in the eleven days of their journey. She gave what she had to the beggars they met; Jean de Metz was always having to hand out money to her for such almsgiving. But more than ever now he felt himself dominated by her. 'Will you be able to do what you say?' he asked. 'I shall do it,' she answered; 'don't fret yourself. My brothers in Paradise and my lord have told me what to do.'

Her language translated the whole feudal system of the Middle Ages to heaven. The vassals of the King of France rode in fealty to the aid of their lord, and with them, vigorous and in masculine clothes, rode the vassal of the King of heaven. She thought in terms of her age; in such events those terms are as good as any, for they meant devotion and speed and clear decision, qualities all of sanctity. So driving through the nights, with the celestial Voices urging her, the group of ardent hearts—'she set me on fire,' said Jean de Metz—came at a charge to Chinon.

At Chinon, however, there was, not unnaturally, a little delay. The Dauphin was there, living poorly—it was said there were not four crowns in the treasury. Still there was the royal household and the Court and

JOAN OF ARC

what remained of the tradition of the French monarchy. It counts for a good deal, in considering Joan, to think that the impression of her energy and sincerity was such that in only two days she was admitted to the Presence. There, however, she met with her first test. She was brought into a hall where fifty torches burned; it was full of lords and gentlemen, some three hundred of them. But the Dauphin was not in the centre; he had put off his cap and stepped aside. A gentleman spoke to her; she took no notice, looked round, saw the Dauphin, went to him, and said in that firm simplicity which distinguished her: 'Most noble lord, I am sent from God to help the kingdom and you.' The Dauphin took her aside; there was private conversation. It was said that she gave him some sign by telling him of a secret thing no one but he knew that he had at heart. He listened; he was moved, but he had to be cautious. He sent her back to her lodgings, and after a few days had her examined by the clergy who were with him. Joan submitted; she was frank with them, but all the while she was clamouring for men, for arms, and for an advance on the enemy. She paid respect to the great personages—dukes and archbishops—among whom she now moved. But it was the young squires and the soldiers of whom she had most hope, as of that squire of the Dauphin whom she clapped on the shoulder, saying it was good to have many such men as he. So when after the careful examinations the prelates asked her whether she could give them a sign that her claims were true, she answered: 'Sign! my sign is to raise the siege of Orleans!'

It was part of the thought of the age that such care

STORIES OF GREAT NAMES

should be taken. For the Middle Ages were based on the supernatural, ever since under the successors of Caesar the Christian Church had come out of the East to Europe, and under Charlemagne and the successors of Charlemagne had established itself and its philosophy as the central idea of Europe. Those ages were accustomed to the possibility of the supernatural in action. But the supernatural might be either good or evil. The Church held that besides the heavenly spirits there were others who were in rebellion against their Creator and God. These rebellious and evil powers also could influence men, and did so influence them to their harm. Witches and sorcerers were in league with the devil and his followers. It was necessary, therefore, that anyone coming with Joan's claims should be examined whether she believed rightly, and behaved rightly. They catechized her carefully, the lords of her Church, or those rather who were of the French party. Cautiously, they declared themselves satisfied; they advised the Dauphin that he might safely use the help she offered.

But what was that help? She was no princess; she had no lands or alliances, money or men. She had had no military training. She had no power to launch thunderbolts on the English army or strike the soldiers with blindness. She had, in fact, nothing but herself, and that, so far as the war went, meant only her passionate belief in her Voices and her mission. The French cause was daily losing ground, however, for lack precisely of some such intense energy of belief and of the drive of action that would result from it. The Dauphin hardly believed in himself or his cause.

JOAN OF ARC

The despairing French in Orleans, the despairing French armies that from a distance watched the English blockade growing tighter, felt themselves failing, in spite of a few admirable generals and courageous leaders. The House of France was on the point of falling, and England and Burgundy would divide the prey. The command was failing. 'My brothers in Paradise and my lord have commanded me,' said Joan. To Orleans !

It was May 1429. The Dauphin, overwhelmed by the girl's confidence and confirmed by the assent of his ecclesiastics and the rising courage of the soldiers who had met her, took the risk and put everything into her hands. He had a suit of armour made for her; he made new efforts to gather a convoy of food for Orleans, and succeeded. The convoy, escorted by what army he had left, set out, and Joan went with it. She was impatient; time had been wasted, and her Voices had commanded her to free France.

She was impatient also in another sense. The French army, like all others at all times, was composed of very many types of soldiers. They drank; they swore; they rioted. Joan, full of goodwill and good humour, the best of comrades and of friends, would not permit what she called sacrilege and sin. The army, half-laughing, half-protesting, but all willingly obedient, found itself wholly reformed. It was not the delicate wistfulness of a remote piety which effected this, but Joan's extremely healthy and extremely determined resolution. One of the French generals protested that he could not manage without swearing; she allowed him, as a concession, to swear ' by my staff '. She had banners made on which Christ was painted; she had hymns sung on the march. Her purity cleansed the army that her energy had created; it swung to its task with a new delight and belief in itself and its purpose, and the strength of her sanctity went over it.

By this time the English had heard of her and of what she was supposed to be doing. It was inevitable that they should not take the same view of her mission as the French. They thought her a witch, but they—or most of them—did not doubt her supernatural powers, and to fight witches, supported by devilish powers, was a more dangerous thing than fighting the dispirited French; more dangerous and more awful. Many, no doubt, were sceptical; they thought the Dauphin had got hold of a popular mascot. Many—for these armies were still more feudal than national—may have wondered whether she might not be a heavenly messenger after all. They talked, all of them, and the army was disturbed and a little alarmed by the new crusade, divine or devilish, which seemed to be launched against them.

The commander of the French forces was Jean, Count de Dunois, lieutenant-general of the kingdom. He, too, had heard of the new-comer and had sent to the King to learn more. His messengers on their return reported to him before the people of Orleans, and a freshness of expectation, such as had not been known for months, arose in the city. A very little was needed now to suggest victory or defeat to the respective armies, and that was supplied. The provisions had been put on boats in order that they might enter the

JOAN OF ARC

city without the army having to fight the English. This, however, depended on the wind which was blowing down the river and away from the town. Joan who had joined Dunois protested against this method, but while they were talking the wind changed. The boats, with its help sailed up the river, and in face of the English army entered the town.

As soon as the town was thus provisioned, and Joan herself had entered it, she caused a letter to be written to the English dated on ' Tuesday in Holy Week ', bidding them give up to ' the Maid, sent from God ', the French towns in their power. It commanded them to go to their own country. Dunois went to Blois to bring more men. He was back in a few days, and directly afterwards the grand attack on the English lines was made. The English had been showing a new tendency to keep within their own fortifications. Dunois declared that up to then the English could put to flight four or five times their number of French, but that then the odds turned, and five hundred or so French could dismay the whole English army. The moral strength of the armies had changed over. It is not therefore surprising that from that hour the recovery of France began.

There was a grand victory and the blockade was broken. Joan, who went among the fighting, though she used no weapons, and only carried her banner— Christ with an angel bearing the lily of France—had been wounded. She recovered quickly, however, and she and Dunois urged the Dauphin to press on with the war. After what had happened the Maid's request was decisive. The armies moved ; the victories continued. Joan rode with her soldiers. Once, when the English force offered battle, Dunois and the other captains asked Joan what she advised. She answered, speaking so loudly that many could hear her : ' Have you good spurs ? ' ' What ! are we to retreat ? ' the captains asked in surprise. ' No,' she said joyously, ' it's the English who will run ; you will need good spurs to follow them.' It happened as she said.

This fighting, however, had a particular object. Joan had had from the beginning one general aim and two particular. The general aim was to free France ; the particular were to raise the siege of Orleans and to have the Dauphin crowned King of France at Rheims. This city was the holy place of the French monarchy. Until any King of France had been crowned there he scarcely seemed to be King ; once he had, the sacred authority of the kingship came upon him. To achieve this coronation was, as Joan saw it, the extreme and the limit of her mission. She was to restore, in that sense, the kingship to France ; once that was done, her business was done. The enemies of the King would gradually fail, and presently be quite beyond doing any injury to him or to his realm. Orleans had been saved ; there remained Rheims.

She achieved it. She forced the leaders of the army to abandon this or that strategic plan, and to adopt hers which was meant to clear the road to Rheims. The tall figure in white armour, carrying the banner, appeared outside one after another of the English holds. Once, in storming a town, she had mounted on a scaling ladder, carrying her banner, when she was knocked to the ground by a stone. She raised herself, and cried

JOAN OF ARC

out : 'Come on, friends! the English are in our hands for our Lord has judged them! Courage and come on!' Once when the Duke d'Alençon, the King's brother, hesitated over some order to attack which she had impetuously issued, she called to him: 'Are you afraid, beau sire? Do you not know that I promised your wife I would bring you safely back to her?' It was in the same high spirit of humility that, when men praised her deeds and said that no clerk had ever read such things in any book, she answered: 'My lord has a book in which no clerk has ever read, however perfect a clerk he may be.'

By such means she brought the Dauphin to Rheims where, with all ancient ceremonial, he was crowned. 'And always', wrote a contemporary, 'during that mystery the Maid stood next the King, her standard in her hand. A right fair thing it was to see the goodly manners of the King and the Maid.' After the ceremony she fell on her knees, and embracing the King's knees, broke into tears of joy, saying: 'Gentle King, now the Will of God is done.' France had again a King, but, and now, in a sense, for the first time the King had France; a nation was rising, and the forces which were being driven out by that nation were forming into another, partly compacted by those very blows. Joan had done the things she set out to do. There was a darker phrase which was sometimes on her lips, she said—the Duke d'Alençon heard her—that she would last a year and no more, and it was for the King to consider how to employ that year. She had arrived at Chinon on Sunday, 6 March 1429; she had started from Orleans on 27 April, and the siege had been raised

on 8 May. The Dauphin had been crowned on 17 July.
Her catastrophe was to begin on 23 May 1430, thirteen
months from her first march with the army.

In fact, however, she did not wish to remain even
for the year of which she spoke. After the coronation
she begged the King to let her go back to Domremy.
She asked for no reward for herself. Her father came
to Rheims for the coronation ; his expenses were paid
and a gift sent him. The town of Domremy by her
request was exempted from taxes. The King, without
her request, granted a coat of arms to her brothers ;
that is, as we should say, he knighted them, or at least
raised them to the rank of knights. But she had—
what she wished—nothing ; and she was denied what
she wished—that is, to go home. They desired to keep
her, for luck ; but, if we must talk of luck, we must say
her luck had left her. If we talk in the terms that she
herself used, we must say that her Voices spoke
truthfully, when they told her what she was to do,
how long her time would last, and when later they said
to her : ' You will be taken ; do not be troubled ;
thus it must be.'

The political situation had now entirely changed, and
the diplomats began to take control. Since they would
not let her go, she begged the King to march, or let her
march, on Paris. At first the King assented ; she led
an assault on it, and was wounded. Then the King
changed his mind. Negotiations had been opened with
the Duke of Burgundy, who under cover of these
negotiatic   passed by the French and entered Paris,
holding it in alliance with the English generals. It was
after this that ' the will of the Maid and the armies of

JOAN OF ARC

the King were broken '. Before her retreat she hung up in the Church of St. Denis the sword and armour she had used during the early part of her career; she had others, but it was a moment of division, almost of separation. It was September 1429.

Through the winter the political moves went on. Joan was kept with the armies, almost like an encouraging show, but very little was allowed to happen. This in itself is not particularly to the discredit of the King and his government, who preferred if possible to recover all they could by negotiation, to make friends with Burgundy, and to make an opportunity for settling the kingdom in a little military and financial peace. Joan and they agreed, from different points of view, celestial and political, that her period of real usefulness was over. But they could not bring themselves to let her go, and there may have been a vague feeling that it was safer to keep a person of her sort under their eyes and in the intangible bonds of their own activities. There was no telling what she might do or what her Voices might suggest to her in the remote fields of Domremy.

It was May 1430. The English party were engaged in counteracting the effect of the Dauphin's coronation by arranging another on their side. The young Henry VI, son of Henry V of Agincourt, had been brought over to France, and was to be crowned at Paris.' Joan, still desiring that her party should abandon discussion, and fling themselves in arms against their enemies, heard that the strong place of Compiegne was in difficulties. She rode by night to its help. She reached the town and secretly entered it in the early morning. At five in the afternoon she led the defenders in a sudden sally. The sally scattered a Burgundian outpost, but other enemy forces came up. Three times she charged and drove them back. But English soldiers, hurrying up, came between her and the town. She and a few of her people were driven off the road on to meadows that were half marsh. Her enemies thronged round her. An archer caught at her and pushed her from her horse; her friends could not get to her to remount her, for they themselves were being overcome. Someone called on her to surrender; she refused: 'I have sworn to another than you, and I will keep my word!' She was seized at last, and carried off among yells of triumph to the enemy's camp.

'You will be taken; do not be troubled; thus it must be.'

She was a person of far too much importance to be left to her immediate captors; she was handed over to the great lords of the opposite party, first to 'my lord of Luxembourg'. But now she who had been celestial had become infernal; the other side of the supernatural hypothesis had her in its grip. She was a witch, and now, it seemed to her enemies, her master the devil had forsaken her as he always forsakes, and betrayed her as he always betrays, those who are miserable and wicked enough to be his servants. The exultant letters of the Duke of Burgundy proclaimed the news to the world.

It was a year and three months since she had set out from Vaucouleurs for Chinon. It was to be a year and a week before her agony was ended; so closely equal

JOAN OF ARC

is the tale of her leadership, actual or formal, and her captivity. For some months she remained in the power of Jean de Luxembourg, and as Jean de Metz had brought her to the King of France so Jean de Luxembourg sold her to the English.

She was to be destroyed. But it is not to be thought that that decision was entirely made before the trial or the trial will be misunderstood. She was a prisoner of war, but she could not be dealt with as an ordinary prisoner of war, and either held for ransom or held as a captive without ransom. Ransom was a part of the habits of the Middle Ages. Richard I of England ransomed himself; so, in the very age of Joan, did Charles Duke of Orleans. But the King of France offered no ransom for Joan, nor is it likely the English would have accepted it. The terms which Joan herself had declared to be the terms upon which she acted forbade that. She had claimed to come from ' her lord ' by direct command from great beings who were her superiors in the feudal hierarchy of heaven, and yet themselves vassals to the supreme suzerainty of God. She said she had been sent by the Church triumphant. But neither the lords of France nor the lords of England had any claim to decide such claims. Only the lords of the Church militant—the doctors, the theologians, the bishops—could decide such a question. It was to their decision that she was brought. She was carried to Rouen and set on her trial for heresy and impiety before the Bishop of Beauvais.

Any organized religion regards such enthusiasts as Joan with scepticism and mistrust—and not unjustly, for against every sincere and holy soul such as Joan there are a hundred who thrust themselves forward because of egotism, or greed, or insanity. Joan herself had had to deal with pretenders of that type, and others appeared in the French camp soon after her capture. They, and those like them, did great harm. It is to the credit of the ecclesiastical authorities that they discouraged all such sin and madness. It is less to their credit—it is, in turn, their sin—that they allowed themselves to be dominated by their circumstances, especially by the English lords. Joan was kept, not in the prisons of the Church—to which she asked to be moved—but in a cell where, chained day and night, she had by day and night the company of a guard of five soldiers of the Earl of Warwick. Her examinations were manipulated in the interests of the English party, and deliberately falsified; so that she was said to have invoked spirits whereas her whole evidence was that she had not invoked them. She appealed both to the Pope and to the General Council of the Church; both appeals were neglected.[1] She referred to her earlier examinations by the clergy of the other side; no notice was taken of them.

The trial lasted almost a year. They catechized her continuously, and she answered as she had answered all those five years since the Voice came to her in her father's garden. But the slow torture of question and captivity, of insult and mockery, wore her down. She heard her Voices still; they promised her victory at last. She said they had

[1] It is however true that if the appeal of everyone accused before the Church courts to the Pope had to be allowed, the whole system would have broken down. Much more so if every accused heretic's case had to be decided by a General Council.

JOAN OF ARC

promised that she should be free in three months ; in three months she was certainly free from all mortal agony. On 9 May 1430 her judges threatened her with physical torture ; she was shown the instruments, the executioners standing by. But she could say nothing more ; she could not deny her Voices or declare that they were from devils, or reject her belief that she had been in obedience to God. It was voted by her judges that she should not be tortured—by eleven votes to three.

At last they brought her to the choice—on a platform, in the market-place of St. Ouen : to abjure or to burn. They began to read her sentence to her when she interrupted them : ' she would hold what her judges decreed, she would obey, she would not uphold the revelations.' Round the two platforms on which she and her accusers stood a tumult broke out. The soldiery thought she was escaping from death ; stones were thrown. The priests ran to her with an abjuration for her to sign. She signed. Obedience had sent her to France ; between that obedience and the other obedience which the judges were now demanding she for a moment wavered, and uncertain of what her Voices meant she signed. She was reported to have said that her Voices had told her what she would do. But they had said also, when she asked them if she would be burned : ' Wait upon our Lord, and He will be your help.'

The sentence of excommunication and death was revoked ; she was sentenced only to lifelong imprisonment and penance—she who was then nineteen years old. She was carried back to the prison from which she had been brought, to the cell, the chains, the English soldiers. It was against all the rules of the Church now, as it had been all through the trial. The great, the only, blame that the authorities of the Church bear through the whole dreadful business is that they did not behave as authorities of the Church.

All this time she had been wearing, as she had done since she left Vaucouleurs, male dress. But as a sign of her penitence she was now to wear woman's dress again. It was brought to her and she put it on. It was 24 May 1430. She was left in the prison and under the old guard. On 27 May the judges in the castle above were told that she was again wearing her male dress. They went to her and found that it was so. It was enough for them. She was declared ' a relapsed heretic ', and as quickly as might be, on 29 May, she was convicted and sentenced ; on 30 May she was to be put to death.

On the morning of her martyrdom she received the Sacrament of our Lord. Then she was put again in woman's dress and carried to the market-place of Rouen. The sentence was read. She listened ; she called out on God and the Saints. The soldiers round the scaffold shouted to the bishop and clergy : ' Do you want to keep us here for dinner ? ' She was hurried to the great heap of faggots, and the stake rising above them ; she was bound to it. She cried on St. Catherine and St. Michael, prince of angels. They lit the faggots. She cried with a great voice, ' Jesus ! ' and so died.

In 1436 the English lost Paris ; in 1439 they lost Normandy ; by 1453 they held nothing in France but Calais. In 1450-6 a Trial of Rehabilitation was held in France, and Joan was declared free from all censure. In 1920 she in her turn was canonized—declared to have been of holy life, and now worthy to be invoked and adored by all Christian people, a right companion of Catherine and Margaret and the archangel who had called to her in the garden of Domremy.

WILLIAM SHAKESPEARE

WILLIAM SHAKESPEARE was born in Stratford-on-Avon. He was baptized on 26 April 1564, but the day of his birth is uncertain. A pleasant, but unreliable, tradition fixed it as 23 April, St. George's day, on which day he died in 1616. He was then 52.

It was not a very long life; it was not even a very remarkable life, or at least the remarks made about it at the time were something less than striking. So far as can be seen it consisted of passing through the ordinary experiences of man, of writing certain plays and poems, of making a certain fair reputation, and of accumulating a moderate fortune. There is no record to show that his exterior life was not as conventional as any of his time. Of his interior life we know nothing except what we choose to deduce from his work. But it must be recognized that it is our deduction and not his information that gives us the clue.

He belonged to what then corresponded to a lower middle-class family of the present day. Stratford was a provincial market-town, standing chiefly on the north bank of the River Avon, in Warwickshire, in the very centre of England. A stone bridge crossed the river; the town consisted of several large streets besides a number of smaller. The houses were said to be ' reasonably well builded of timber ', with a good many trees, especially elms, around and between them. Beyond the town lay forest and open fields. Two roads

WILLIAM SHAKESPEARE

—not of the first importance—met in it from London; one came from Oxford, the other by Edgehill, famous afterwards as the scene of a battle in the Civil Wars. The population was concerned, on the one hand, with farming and the raising of live stock; on the other, with such semi-agricultural industries as weaving, shoe-making, glove-making, carpentry, etc. The country served the town and the town served the country. It was governed, under a royal charter, by its own officers, a bailiff and a town council. Townspeople had a duty to serve on the council if chosen, and were fined for non-attendance at its meetings. There was a Grammar School, of good standing, and easy communication with the greater world beyond the town. It was a self-contained but not a self-enclosed community, controlled in national affairs by the central Tudor government in London, and affected, if gradually and indirectly, by the great European movements beyond the sea.

John Shakespeare, Shakespeare's father, was not a native of the town. He was a well-to-do burgess, occupying himself with various trade activities, being primarily a glover, but also sometimes concerned with sales of wool, barley, timber. His wife was a certain Mary Arden, related to one of the lesser county families, and a small heiress. They had eight children in all, four girls, three of whom died in childhood, and one Joan, born in 1569, lived, and four sons—William, Gilbert (born in 1566), Richard (1573-4), Edmund (1580). John Shakespeare took at first an active part in the public life of Stratford. Between 1557 and 1564 he held various offices; he was also fined twice for letting the garbage of the house lie in the gutter outside his door. He became alderman in 1565, bailiff in 1568, and chief alderman in 1571.

William therefore passed his first years in the household of an active and prospering family. He had, up to 1571, a younger brother and a very small sister. It is reported that he was sent to the school at Stratford, though he had to be taken away rather earlier than was usual because his father began to lose money and needed the boy's assistance at home. But while he was there he had a good grounding in Latin, learning to speak in it and to read certain Latin writers, especially Ovid. Long afterwards Ben Jonson, his fellow playwright, said of him that ' he had little Latin and less Greek '. But Ben Jonson was an especially learned man for a playwright, and was also a man intensely aware of his own powers. Not to be Jonson's equal—and still more not to be one whom Jonson thought his equal—in knowledge of the classic authors, who made up most of the book-learning of the time, does not necessarily mean any unusual ignorance. The young Shakespeare's early days were passed in the full country of Elizabethan England, in the house of a prosperous tradesman-father and a mother related to the aristocracy, and in a school which was one of the best smaller schools in England. For the development of an active and ingenious mind it was no bad training.

But John Shakespeare failed to keep his position in his world. He sold some of his wife's property and mortgaged the rest. By 1578 he was even failing to pay his taxes and owed (at least) £5 to a Stratford baker. Soon afterwards he ceased to attend the meetings of the Town Council. He was deprived of

WILLIAM SHAKESPEARE

his aldermanship in 1587; the family were going steadily down hill. In 1592 he was named as one of nine persons who were said to ' come not to church for fear of process for debt '.

In the midst of these distresses, William Shakespeare was married. Documents were issued from the offices of the Bishop of Worcester on 27 and 28 November 1582 which permitted the parties to go through the ceremony without banns being called, in the season of Advent when marriages were usually forbidden. The bride—a young woman of 26—was Anne Hathaway, probably of Shottery, a village near Stratford. The formal marriage may have been hastened, since Anne's first child, Susannah, was baptized on 26 May 1583. At 20, therefore, the young William was married and a father; he had to support his household, and he could hope for little help from his own father. It seems he must have been already vividly aware of financial difficulties, and that these must have become more acute when, nearly two years later, twins were born to him. They were baptized on 2 February 1585, and were named Hamnet and Judith, after a baker of Stratford and his wife, Hamnet and Judith Sadler.

This is all our certain knowledge of him at this period. But tales, then or afterwards, got about. It used to be said that he was once apprentice to a butcher, and that he ran away from his master. The story went that ' when he killed a calf he would do it in a high style, and make a speech '. John Shakespeare was said, among other things, to have been a butcher, and even if he did not exercise this trade habitually it is possible enough that there was sometimes need of a

STORIES OF GREAT NAMES

calf-killing, so that such an incident is not impossible. But Sir Edmund Chambers has pointed out that, sixty years before this time, there is a record of some kind of entertainment, presented at least once before royalty, which was called 'killing a calf', so that it is equally possible that the tale is no more than a muddled memory of Shakespeare taking part in rural amusements, and perhaps doing it more theatrically than did others. Another, and more famous, story recounts that he trespassed in the park of Sir Thomas Lucy, a landowner near Stratford, and was proceeded against for deer-stealing. He is said also to have composed a ballad, in revenge, against Lucy, and because of this quarrel to have been compelled to leave Stratford. Something of the sort is not incredible, but in fact we do not know, any more than we know what occupation he followed between 1583 or 1584, when the twins were born, and 1592 when his name is first heard of in London. He has been held to have been a schoolmaster, a lawyer's clerk, an apothecary, a soldier, a printer; to have wandered among Cotswold villages and to have been patronized by great persons. Certainly he disappears from the Stratford records, and where and how he went we cannot tell. It is more easy to guess why. He was young, he was poor, he was capable. He needed and wanted money—as fair and satisfactory a livelihood as he could gain. It was in search of a fortune, which (more fortunate than some lesser poets) he afterwards found, that, at some moment in those years which preceded and followed the coming of the Armada to England in 1587, he first changed and finally settled his career.

WILLIAM SHAKESPEARE

In the year 1592 he was about 28 or 29. In the same year there died in London the poet Robert Greene at about the age of 32. He had been a young fellow who, when he came up to London from Cambridge, had taken to writing plays for the theatres. Much besides plays had come from his pen, poetry and prose, pamphlets of satire upon the fashions of the day and pamphlets of invective against other writers of the day. In this year of his death he had published, of the first kind, *Disputation between a hee Coney Catcher and a shee Conny Catcher*—Conny or Coney Catchers being rascals who got their living by cheating fools and dupes in the public places of London ; and of the second, *A Quip for an Upstart Courtier*. This was a contribution to one of the many literary quarrels which raged then, as they do wherever genius is prevalent and poets are excitable. The theatrical companies of London were, in those years, passing through a bad time. The plague had been about ; some companies had failed ; others had been re-organized. New writers, as always, were coming in ; and old writers, as always, were complaining. Greene, at any rate, felt that the actors for whom he had written, and to whom he believed his plays had been profitable, were scandalously deserting him for other poets. He was poor and miserable ; he was dying. He wrote a last pamphlet : *Greene's Groatsworth of Wit bought with a Million of Repentance* and addressed it *To those Gentlemen his quondam Acquaintances who spend their wits in making plaies*. Of those gentlemen possibly one, and if so certainly the greatest, was Christopher Marlowe, said to have been born in the same year as Shakespeare, and a poet of

STORIES OF GREAT NAMES

perhaps no less genius. But while Shakespeare had been at Stratford Marlowe had been at Cambridge, and like Greene, coming to London, had taken to writing for the stage. This group of poets—Greene and Marlowe and others—were called 'the University wits'; they had held theatres in the power of their genius, and the dying man raged at the ingratitude of men. Other poets were appearing: 'puppets', he wrote fiercely, 'that speak from our mouths . . . antics garnished in our colours,' 'apes' imitating ' your past excellence'. Among those puppets, antics, and apes, those plagiarists whom the 'rude grooms' of the theatre companies were now willing to use instead of his friends, there was one especially who angered him. This new young creature had learned from them the way to write, copying their style, 'beautified with our feathers', and now, 'upstart Crow . . . with his *Tiger's heart wrapt in a Player's hide*,' wrote Greene, catching at a line of the new man's to turn it to a sneer, ' supposes he is as well able to bombast out a blank verse as the best of you : and being an absolute *Johannes fac totum*, is in his own conceit the only Shake-scene in a country.' The pun pointed the allusion.

The Stratford husband then was now in London and already beginning to matter, though by 1592 he had little enough that we can see to his credit. He had, by one means or another, thrust his way into the theatres, had got himself taken on here or there. A later story told how he had begun by holding horses outside one of the theatres; certainly he had not entered them by force of money or reputation. He

WILLIAM SHAKESPEARE

was ' at first in a very mean rank '. But, however he had begun, some intelligent person among the managers of the theatre companies had already recognized his value as a writer and re-writer of plays. The line Greene borrowed is from 3 *Henry VI* ; that play then had already been manipulated by him. His ' bombast' was recognized.

Yet it was not to Greene that Shakespeare's greatest debt was due, but to the other ' University wit ', the Marlowe who was his equal in age and power, and at that moment perhaps more than his equal. It is likely enough that the difference was one of education and circumstance rather than of anything else. Stratford was a good school, but it was not Cambridge ; it was a reasonable town, but it was not London. And now, or recently, while Shakespeare was busy on what work they gave him, Marlowe had rounded and prolonged English blank verse into a new thing in the two parts of *Tamerlane the Great*. Countryman as he might be originally, Shakespeare knew the metropolitan accent of great verse. Greene 'was so far right that Shakespeare's genius knew and rose to what Marlowe and his friends had done. He plagiarized their style, because it was that of his own spirit. He allied himself with that style, and it became his own.

The publisher of Greene's pamphlet, Henry Chettle, discovered that it had caused umbrage in certain quarters ; it had been ' offensively taken '. Greene by now was dead, and Chettle was willing to make courteous amends in a book of his own which he published the same year, *Kind Hart's Dreame*, a not unsuitable title. The kind heart of Chettle addressed itself to the two gentlemen supposed to be chiefly involved ; it is believed the first was Marlowe and the second Shakespeare.

About three months since died Mr. Robert Greene, leaving many papers in sundry booksellers' hands, among other his *Groat's Worth of Wit*, in which a letter written to divers playmakers is offensively by one or two of them taken ; and because on the dead they cannot be avenged, they wilfully forge in their conceits a living author ; and after tossing it to and fro, no remedy but it must light on me. How have I all the time of my conversing in printing, hindered the bitter inveighing against scholars, it has been very well known ; and how in that I dealt I can sufficiently prove. With neither of them that took offence was I acquainted, and with one of them I care not if I never be. The other, whom at that time I did not so much spare, as since I wish I had, for that, as I have moderated the heat of living writers, and might have used my own discretion, especially in such a case, the author being dead, that I did not I am as sorry as if the original fault had been my fault, because my self have seen his demeanour no less civil than he excellent in the quality he professes. Besides, divers of worship have reported his uprightness of dealing, which argues his honesty and his facetious [polished] grace in writing that approves his art.

It seems then that by this point in his career Shakespeare had already a reputation for pleasantness —' affability '—and good-temper as well as for verse-writing. The circle that included poets and publishers on the one hand, however, reached up to include peers on the other, and it was to one of them that, in the years 1593 and 1594, he offered his first, and only,

WILLIAM SHAKESPEARE

essays in work of a different style. Two long, decorative and fashionable poems appeared, each dedicated to the Earl of Southampton with a graceful twist of language —' what I have done is yours, what I have to do is yours, being part in all I have, devoted yours.' So *Lucrece*, the second of the two. Southampton was then a man of twenty-one, a friend of the ' bombastical ' Earl of Essex, Elizabeth's favourite. The relationship between the patron and the poet was common enough at the time, though tales of Southampton's generosity have been exaggerated as if to make him not unworthy of Shakespeare's genius. That genius, however, never showed any reluctance to accept the order of the world and of society. He, like so many of his fellows, realized in that age the need of government and a sturdy commonwealth. It is easy for ours which does not feel his loyalties to attribute them to insincerity or greed. But so far as we do so we are apt to misunderstand not only the man but (what is for us more important) the poetry.

The chief of those loyalties, and one most difficult for modern minds to experience in its fullness of emotion, was that to the Queen. In the year 1594 there appears in the royal accounts the first entry which connects his name with hers—' to William Kempe, William Shakespeare and Richard Burbage servants to the Lord Chamberlain, upon the Council's warrant dated at Whitehall 15th March 1594, for two several Comedies or Interludes, showed by them before Her Majesty in Christmas time last past, viz. upon St. Stephen's Day and Innocents' Day, £13 6s. 7d., and by way of Her Majesty's reward £6 14s. 3d., in all £20.'

STORIES OF GREAT NAMES

There were to be others. Apocryphal stories record her approval of his work, and on occasion her commands for it. Thus it is said that the *Merry Wives of Windsor* is due to her desire for a play showing Falstaff in love, and it is to be hoped she liked what she got. It was all she could get, for the grand and self-sufficient figure of Falstaff was incapable of the self-forgetful humility of real love. Even so, he might have been shown as less defeated by common men, but the tale says that Shakespeare wrote the play in a fortnight to satisfy the Queen, and treated Falstaff badly as a result.

But if sometimes she was a taskmistress to him, she was also a vision. In *A Midsummer-Night's Dream* he put lines which contain an aspect of the vision.

> That very time I saw, but thou couldst not,
> Flying between the cold moon and the earth,
> Cupid all arm'd : a certain aim he took
> At a fair vestal throned by the west,
> And loos'd his love-shaft smartly from his bow,
> As it should pierce a hundred thousand hearts ;
> But I might see young Cupid's fiery shaft
> Quench'd in the chaste beams of the wat'ry moon,
> And the imperial votaress passed on,
> In maiden meditation, fancy-free.

It is quite likely that Shakespeare smiled a little as he finished that. He as much as anyone appreciated the splendour of the tribute, and he lived in London and knew whatever gossip or scandal related of the life of the Queen. But it is impossible to avoid believing that, though he smiled, he meant the verse; you do not create such poetry out of cynical falsehood. Poets

WILLIAM SHAKESPEARE

have a double vision. They can see everything at once in its smallness and its greatness. It was to be the glory of Shakespeare's final poetic style that, more than any other English poet, he achieved the power of saying things which were as many-sided as the facts to which they alluded—which were at once comic, tragic, and ironic, and yet none of these adjectives are sufficient for his lines, because they, like the things, are all of them from different aspects, and none is sufficient for all.

Thus in the year 1595 he had fully entered on his career. He was no longer a ' hired man ' in the theatre; he had bought, perhaps with some gift from the Earl of Southampton, a share in the company of actors known as the Lord Chamberlain's men. He was therefore, on the financial side, a person of standing in his theatre. On the poetic side he had ceased any hack work upon which he had originally been employed; he had finished with his own earlier immaturity. The spectacular wickedness of *Richard III*, the stagy boisterousness of the *Comedy of Errors*, and the *Taming of the Shrew*, the sheer bloody wildness of *Titus Andronicus*, all these lay behind him. His verse was rising into the rich fullness of *Romeo*, of *Richard II*, of *A Midsummer Night's Dream*. There were many other poets writing all around him; he was but one, though among the best. Yet to us, looking back, he is curiously alone, for his great young rival was dead. In 1593 Marlowe had fallen under the dagger at an inn in Deptford. *Dr. Faustus* would have no successor, and Shakespeare no near other star.

He lived then a figure marked, if not prominent, in his world, and, to whatever profundities of poetry his developing imagination pierced, he never lost touch with his world. It may even be hoped that, so far as any man can, he enjoyed it. There was never a poet, so far as we can judge from what records remain, less a 'dreamer', less the inefficient stray of fancy on a harsh poetical earth, than Shakespeare. He was doubly competent—to a double business; he made poetry and also he made money. But he did both at once, and it was his one mind which he gave to both; now refusing to be defeated by the most extreme crisis of the human mind, now declining to be cheated of his dues by a Stratford tradesman. He was at the service of his fellows—it is shown by a certain lawsuit in which he was a witness; but he did not propose to put himself utterly at their mercy. Perhaps a greater saint might have acted differently, but Shakespeare was not a saint, or at least there is no anecdote to suggest it. A minor poet of the next century, Abraham Cowley, wrote of another poet as much greater than he as less than Shakespeare, Richard Crashaw :—

> Poet and Saint ! to thee alone are given
> The two most sacred Names of Earth and Heaven.
> The hard and rarest Union which can be
> Next that of Godhead with Humanitie.

So much could hardly be said of our supreme master. Yet, as far as we can understand, reading the plays and studying the records, he carried humanity to its loftiest power short of that sanctity. But he never forgot that he lived in the world.

Of the year 1596 we know of two incidents. One was an application made to the Herald's Office for a

WILLIAM SHAKESPEARE

coat of arms for the family. It had been an old dream
of his father's, almost thirty years before, and now the
son assisted in the fulfilment. Rash minds have
supposed this to indicate a kind of snobbery in the poet.
But, even if we suppose that he took a vivid personal
interest in the application and was not only carrying
out his father's wishes, there is no need to think
anything of the kind. The plays are full of an intense
delight in such significant pageantry, in colour and
diagram, in office and richness. Sometimes his kings,
who have to endure too much consciousness of those
things revile them, as Henry V does.

> And what have kings that privates have not too,
> Save ceremony, save general ceremony?
> And what art thou, thou idle ceremony?
> What kind of god art thou, thou suffer'st more
> Of mortal griefs than do thy worshippers?
> What are thy rents? What are thy comings-in?
> O ceremony! show me but thy worth:
> What is thy soul or adoration?
> Art thou aught else but place, degree, and form,
> Creating awe and fear in other men?
> Wherein thou art less happy, being fear'd,
> Than they in fearing.
> What drink'st thou oft, instead of homage sweet,
> But poison'd flattery? O! be sick, great greatness,
> And bid thy ceremony give thee cure.
> Think'st thou the fiery fever will go out
> With titles blown from adulation?
> Will it give place to flexure and low-bending?
> Canst thou, when thou command'st the beggar's knee,
> Command the health of it? No, thou proud dream,
> That play'st so subtly with a king's repose;

STORIES OF GREAT NAMES

> I am a king that find thee; and I know
> 'Tis not the balm, the sceptre and the ball,
> The sword, the mace, the crown imperial,
> The intertissued robe of gold and pearl,
> The farced title running 'fore the king,
> The throne he sits on, nor the tide of pomp
> That beats upon the high shore of this world,
> No, not all these, thrice-gorgeous ceremony,
> Not all these, laid in bed majestical,
> Can sleep so soundly as the wretched slave, . . .

But the poet who so reviled ceremony on Henry's behalf had certainly a very real apprehension of ceremony, and the ceremonial of arms was within his reach. It was part of the splendour of the age. It may be supposed that Shakespeare did not overvalue them; neither did he undervalue them. They were a part of his world, and he accepted the conditions of his world. ' Honour lay in his way, and he found it.'

In the same year he first, in his adult years, knew death in the household at Stratford. His son Hamnet died. ' Sentiment,' said Sir Edmund Chambers, ' would trace a reflection of the event in the sympathetic treatment of Arthur in *King John*, which chronology at least does not forbid.' The reference is to Act III, Scene 4, lines 93-7 :—

> Grief fills the room up of my absent child,
> Lies in his bed, walks up and down with me,
> Puts on his pretty looks, repeats his words,
> Remembers me of all his gracious parts,
> Stuffs out his vacant garments with his form:

There is another possibility of tracing the event. Sir Edmund suggests that ' the bulk of the Sonnets lie

WILLIAM SHAKESPEARE

round 1593-6 '. The opening Sonnets of the series invite some young nobleman to marry, that he may have a child. But afterwards the series grows darker and contemplates the destructiveness and misery which exist in life. This change, which is generally ascribed to differences arising between Shakespeare and his noble friend, is no doubt justly so treated. But his mind, round about that time, was approaching a change of temper. The minds of most men do so change in middle life. But they change under influences, and the death of the boy Hamnet may have been one. It would be as tempting, but more rash, to think that it was the similarity of name which had a part in directing Shakespeare's mind to the story of Hamlet, Prince of Denmark, composed perhaps somewhere about 1600. But four years is a long time, and too many plays of a different kind intervene.

Meanwhile the death of his male heir did not turn his thoughts from the town where he had been born and educated, and where his family lived. His growing fortune enabled him to lay out money in property, and he chose to buy house-property at Stratford. There stood in the centre of the town a fine house and garden, originally built, a century earlier, by a gentleman of rank, Sir Hugh Clopton. It had been sold and bought since then, and now it was again ' in the market '. Shakespeare began negotiations to purchase it. While the transaction was going through, the owner died. The darker side of the Elizabethan age covers that moment, for he had been poisoned by his son. The property passed, not to the criminal, but through him to a second son, and it was from him that Shakespeare

STORIES OF GREAT NAMES

eventually purchased it. Five years later he added to his holdings a cottage in an adjoining lane, and a stretch of open ground in the fields beyond—a hundred and seven acres of arable and twenty acres of pasture.

His relations with the townspeople varied. In 1598 he was engaged, with others of the richer men of Stratford, on something very like a corner in malt. It is true that he was also busy on writing *Henry IV* and *Henry V*, and probably *Much Ado about Nothing*. The poorer folk of the town were engaged on what must have seemed to them much ado about something. There had been several rainy summers, harvests had been spoiled, and the result was a rise in prices. So disturbed did conditions grow that the Queen's Council in London, and even the great Lord Burleigh himself, among his other anxieties, had to take notice of it. They sent instructions to the Justices of the Peace to make inquiry who of the town's inhabitants were holding on to corn, barley, or malt, in hope of a further rise in price; they remarked that among these ' wicked people . . . like to wolves or cormorants ' were ' men which are of good livelihood and in estimation of worship.' The Justices were exhorted to take steps, and in effect, between pressure from the Council and from the populace who were spreading wild rumours that the Earl of Essex would come and hang the ' maltsters ' at their own doors, they found themselves forced to make a return of those responsible. It is in this return that Shakespeare was recorded as having in store ' x quarters ' of malt. Anyone who cannot imagine that a great poet could be guilty of such an anti-social act may perhaps imagine that it was done

WILLIAM SHAKESPEARE

without his knowledge by whoever was representing him at Stratford, even if it were his wife Anne. But there is the record. It seems no further steps were taken.

He himself was probably in London at the time; it was 4 February 1598—in the winter when the theatres were open. A letter exists, from one townsman of Stratford to another, then in London, saying that there is a report that ' our countryman, Mr. Shaksper ', has money to invest, and is thinking of buying some land. The writer goes on to suggest another method of laying it out—buying up some tithes (which, in fact, Shakespeare later did): will his friend see what can be done? He ends up in dog-Latin, and even quotes Virgil: ' Hic labor, hoc opus esset eximiae et gloriae et laudis sibi.' Towards the end of the same year, the London visitor himself drafted a letter to Shakespeare, asking for a loan, though it seems possible the request was never sent.

Loving countryman, I am bold of you as of a friend, craving your help with £30 upon Mr. Busshel's and my security or Mr. Mytton's with me. Mr. Rosswell is not come to London as yet and I have especial cause. You shall friend me much in helping me out of all the debts I owe in London, I thank God, and much quiet my mind which would not be indebted. I am now towards the Court in hope of answer for the dispatch of my business. You shall neither lose credit nor money by me, the Lord willing, and now but persuade yourself so as I hope, and you shall not need to fear but with all hearty thankfulness I will hold my time and content your friend, and if we bargain further you shall be the paymaster yourself. My time bids me hasten to an end and so I commit this to your care and hope of your help. I fear I shall not be back this night from the Court. Haste. The Lord be with you and with us all, Amen. From the Bell in Carter Lane the 25 October 1598. Yours in all kindness Ryc. Quyney.

Richard's father was writing to him five days later :—

You shall, God willing, receive from your wife by the bailiff, this bringer, assurance of 10s. . . . If you bargain with Mr. Sha . . . or receive money therefor, bring your money home if you may. I see how knit stockings be sold, there is great buying of them at Evesham. Edward Wheat and Harry, your brother man, were both at Evesham this day sennight, and, as I heard, bestow £20 there in knit hosings, wherefore I think you may do good if you can have money.

and another friend :—

Your letter of the 25 October came to my hands the last of the same at night per Grenway, which imported . . . that our countryman Mr. Wm. Shak. would procure us money, which I will like of as I shall hear when and where and how ; and I pray let not go that occasion if it may sort to any indifferent conditions. Also that if money might be had for £30 or £40, a lease, etc., might be procured. . . . From Stratford, 4 November 1598 . . . Abrah. Sturley.

On the other hand Shakespeare continued to watch his own financial interests in Stratford. In 1604 he brought an action against one Philip Rogers an apothecary for debt, and against other debtors in 1608-9. He bought a lease of the tithes in 1604, and gradually accumulated more property. It is clear that, outside London, his chief concern was with his own town and his own people.

WILLIAM SHAKESPEARE

It was in London, however, that, from 1598 till about 1613, his career was still continuing. Before that date he had been living in St. Helen's Ward, Bishopsgate ; we know it because he twice did not pay his taxes at the proper time—in 1596 and in 1598. He moved about this time to another lodging on the other side of the Thames in Southwark, and the debts (one of 5s., one of 13s. 4d.) had to be referred by one set of tax-collectors to another. It seems that by 1601 they had managed to extract payment, and the record in their books was cancelled.

About the same time came what was perhaps the most dangerous corner that Shakespeare ever had occasion to turn. During the malt episode at Stratford, or about that time, he had been working on *Henry V*, in which he inserted, as was his habit occasionally, a compliment to Elizabeth, and (in this case) to her favourite the Earl of Essex.

> Were now the general of our gracious empress,—
> As in good time he may,—from Ireland coming,
> Bringing rebellion broached on his sword,
> How many would the peaceful city quit
> To welcome him!

Had Essex returned from Ireland so, all would have been well. In fact, he returned against the Queen's command and was immediately out of favour. The Queen's displeasure, the intrigues of the Court, and his own folly, drove him into conspiracy which soon promised to break out into open rebellion. On 6 February 1601 some of the gentlemen who were supporting him went to the Globe Theatre in Southwark where the Chamberlain's Men were acting and asked

STORIES OF GREAT NAMES

that there should be a special performance on the next afternoon of *Richard II*. The manager to whom they spoke was Augustine Phillipps, one of the company, who demurred to the request. He and his fellows protested that it was an old play, and that a revival would not draw much of an audience. If Shakespeare was among those consulted it is hardly to be doubted that he took this view; he was not the kind of man to whom poetic pride would be compensation for an empty theatre. The gentlemen, however, urged their request, and eventually offered to pay—a fee of forty shillings was mentioned and agreed on, and on the Saturday afternoon the play was presented, including the deposition scene, which though it had probably been acted in 1595 had not been printed, and indeed was not until 1608.

> Now mark me how I will undo myself:
> I give this heavy weight from off my head,
> And this unwieldy sceptre from my hand,
> The pride of kingly sway from out my heart;
> With mine own tears I wash away my balm,
> With mine own hands I give away my crown,
> With mine own tongue deny my sacred state,
> With mine own breath release all duteous rites:
> All pomp and majesty I do forswear;
> My manors, rents, revenues, I forgo;
> My acts, decrees, and statutes I deny:
> God pardon all oaths that are broke to me!
> God keep all vows unbroke are made to thee!

We do not of course know whether those actual lines were repeated, but something like them must have taken place. It was on that very day, perhaps while

WILLIAM SHAKESPEARE

the performance was taking place at the Globe, that messengers from the Queen's Council were asking questions of the Earl of Essex, at Essex House across the river. It was on the next day, a Sunday, that the Earl broke out of his house and came riding through the city, calling on his friends to rise and follow him. The rebellion collapsed; the Earl was taken; Augustine Phillipps was invited by the Council to explain how it happened that so apposite a play had been presented. He seems to have done so satisfactorily, for his examination took place on 18 February, and his company were at court on 24 February. Neither Cecil nor the Queen pressed the matter against them. But it is likely to have given everyone of the company some wakeful moments during the nights of 8 February onwards.

With the accession of James I their popularity at court continued. A few records of it may be noted; one or two are curious in our eyes. On 10 February 1605 which was Shrove Sunday, as it was called, the Sunday before the six weeks fast of Lent, the *Merchant of Venice* was given; on the Monday, a play called the *Spanish Marriage*, but on the Tuesday, by King James's own royal request, they did the *Merchant* again. Let us give that much underrated monarch credit for his taste. In the same year Burbage was commanded to supply a play for private performance before the Queen at the Earl of Southampton's, but he had to report that there was no new one that she had not seen, and the best that could be done was to revive *Love Labour's Lost* which (he assured the gentlemen responsible) ' for wit and mirth will please her exceedingly'. A more surprising arrangement was that by which on the

STORIES OF GREAT NAMES

evening of Boxing Day 1606, as a part of the Christmas revels at court, the King's Men presented *King Lear*. The choice is on a level with the later production of *Othello* as part of the marriage festivities of James's daughter Elizabeth in February 1613. It all seems very odd. But *Othello* was played and Elizabeth was married.

Dim visions of other performances float across the past, prophetic of Shakespeare's later and wider fame. In 1607 there were three ships on the high seas, the *Dragon*, the *Hector*, and the *Consent*, bound for the East Indies. By 5 September of that year they were off Sierra Leone, and there on the *Dragon* a performance of *Hamlet* was given, at which a certain Christianized negro, a relative of the local king, acting as interpreter, was present. Three weeks later *Richard the Second* was presented before Captain Keeling of the *Dragon* and Captain Hawkins of the *Hector*. Much later, but still during the voyage, *Hamlet* was again given before the same two captains, Keeling having first invited Hawkins to 'a fish dinner'. Such performances, Keeling wrote in his log, ' I permit to keep my people from idleness and unlawful games, or sleep.' It will be observed that he was among the first to regard Shakespeare as being morally useful. But he had some excuse.

Meanwhile the poet's own career went on quietly enough. The alteration of the Chamberlain's men to be the King's occasionally brought him into ceremonial prominence, which (other things being equal) he probably enjoyed. They were officers of the royal household, sworn as Grooms of the Chamber, but without payment. At the time of the state entry of

WILLIAM SHAKESPEARE

James into London they received each 4½ yards of scarlet red cloth for new clothes; when the Constable of Castile came to London on an embassy, twelve of them, including Shakespeare, were in attendance as King James's servants. There was a tale (of some authority) that Lady Pembroke wishing to intercede for Sir Walter Raleigh, then in prison, told her son the Earl of Pembroke, to try and persuade James to visit their house near Salisbury, and offered a performance of *As You Like It* as an inducement, adding further: ' We have the man Shakespeare with us.' And *Macbeth* may have partially owed the effectiveness of its witches to the general knowledge of the King's belief in the existence of such terrible spiritual dangers, and certainly owes something of its vision of the kings who ' two-fold balls and treble sceptres carry ' to the King's own royalty, of Scotland, England, and Ireland, and to his well-known passion for the legal union of the realms. Thus the actual facts of Shakespeare's age contributed to the intensity of his imagination; and the achievement of King James to the awful futility of Macbeth.

A few glimpses remain of Shakespeare in less exalted relationships. We know little of his concerns with his fellow-writers. He remembered Marlowe; the reference is in *As You Like It* (*c.* 1599-1600), six years after Marlowe's death, to a line from his *Hero and Leander*

> Dead shepherd, now I find thy saw of might:
> ' Who ever lov'd that lov'd not at first sight ? '

He was friendly with Ben Jonson (born 1573, and thus some nine years younger), though Jonson, whose style of writing was very different from Shakespeare's, was critical of his friend in some things, and had a low opinion of his academic learning. But then Jonson (as has been said) was unusually well-read in Greek and Latin, and had no small idea of his capacities as of himself. There is a wide difference between imagining immortality in your verse for your verse, as Shakespeare did in the Sonnets, and thinking yourself a generally noteworthy person as seems to have been Jonson's habit. It is said that the friendship began with Shakespeare's recognition of Jonson's genius, when by chance he came across a manuscript of the younger poet's that had been submitted. It was about to be returned, ' with an ill-natur'd answer that it would be of no service to their company, when Shakespeare luckily cast his eye upon it,' and prevented by his own admiration and action the abrupt refusal. He acted in Jonson's *Every Man in his Humour* (1598), which may have been the play in question, and in his *Sejanus* (1603). There are different reports of his capacity as an actor; it remained a tradition that he took the part of the Ghost in *Hamlet*, of Adam in *As You Like It*, and (perhaps) of some kings. This does not look as if he were much more than adequate on the stage. It is very possible that, though he could write, he could not rant the great Elizabethan verse satisfactorily enough for the ' groundlings '. There are occasional tributes to his pleasantness and wit in conversation; he moves, in that shadowy world, the most courteous shadow of them all.

One example of that courtesy lingers in the law-records. At one time, *c.* 1603-4, he had lodgings in the

WILLIAM SHAKESPEARE

house of a French Huguenot refugee, named Christopher Mountjoy, a wigmaker who lived at the corner of Silver Street, in Cripplegate, in the north-west part of the city, not very far from Bread Street where, in 1608, John Milton was born in the house of the lawyer his father. In the same house lived Mountjoy's French apprentice, Stephen Bellot. Mountjoy at that time had a sufficiently high opinion of Bellot to plan a marriage between his own daughter Mary and the apprentice. His wife talked of it to Shakespeare, and suggested that he might speak of it to Bellot and urge him to consider the proposal, which Shakespeare seems to have done. There had been ' a show of goodwill ' between the young people, but with a vigilance characteristic both of the Elizabethans and the French, Bellot was anxious to find out what dowry Mountjoy would give with his daughter. During the talks between him and Shakespeare a sum (Shakespeare later thought it might have been £50) was mentioned, and after further discussion the marriage took place. But a few years afterwards Mountjoy, who seems to have been a mildish kind of person for a French Huguenot, had not paid, and in 1612 Bellot brought an action against his father-in-law for money and stuff due to him. By then Shakespeare, at 49 or so, had left London and was living again at Stratford. He came up, however, to Westminster where the Court was sitting, and gave evidence, but on the financial side he had no very clear remembrance. He remembered that Mountjoy had approved of Bellot, he remembered Mrs. Mountjoy involving him in the affair, he remembered the discussions. But he would not swear to any exact sum,

STORIES OF GREAT NAMES

'What sum it was that Mr. Mountjoy promised to give them he the said Mr. Shakespeare could not remember, but said it was £50 or thereabouts to his best remembrance. And as he remembereth Mr. Shakespeare said he promised to give them a portion of his goods: but what, or to what value he remembereth not. And more he cannot depose.' Eventually the case was passed on to the chief men of the Huguenot Church in London, who gave judgement in favour of Bellot.

By 1612 therefore we can assume that Shakespeare had no longer a London address; he was described as 'of Stratford upon Avon in the County of Warwick gentleman'. New Place and his Stratford interests had received him, though he was still doing some work for his old company. His father had died in 1601; his mother in September 1608. But another generation was already in being, for in 1607 Shakespeare's eldest daughter Susanna had married a distinguished doctor, John Hall, and their daughter Elizabeth was baptized on 21 February 1608. There were, of course, troubles at Stratford as there had been in London. Susanna in 1613 brought an action against another Stratford inhabitant who had spread slanderous tales about her, and won her case. There was a good deal of bother about a matter of enclosures in which Shakespeare was so far involved as to come to a private agreement with a neighbouring family to protect his own interests. There is a record of a supply of sack and claret sent in the usual way by the Corporation to New Place, when a minister had come to preach in Stratford and was entertained by Shakespeare. He still maintained his

WILLIAM SHAKESPEARE

interest in property; in 1613 he bought, and mortgaged, a house in Blackfriars, in London.

His other daughter Judith married on 10 February 1616 one of the Quyny family, a certain Thomas, a vintner. Soon afterwards, in March, her father was engaged upon drawing up his will, for which he had apparently given earlier instruction. Sir Edmund Chambers summarizes it as follows :—

There are small bequests to the poor, to various Stratfordians, and to Shakespeare's 'fellows' Burbadge, Heminges, and Condell, who are to buy rings. Thomas Combe, the brother of William, is to have Shakespeare's sword. The widow, amply provided for by legal dower on the Stratford property, although that on the Blackfriars house had been barred, gets the second best bed by an interlineation. Joan Hart is to occupy her present house, which was one of those in Henley St., for life, and to have £20 and the poet's wearing apparel. Each of her three sons gets £5. Subject to certain contingencies, another £150 later. She is also to have a silver and gilt bowl. The rest of the plate is for Elizabeth Hall; the other chattels and the leases for her parents. The real property in Stratford and London is entailed successively upon Susanna and her heirs male, Judith and her heirs male, with remainder to the poet's right heirs.

The will was signed on 25 March 1616. During the next month (according to a reliable report) Shakespeare had a meeting with two of his old friends—Michael Drayton and Ben Jonson; it may be that they were both staying in Stratford for a night or more. They drank together merrily, as they had so often done. But during the meeting Shakespeare caught a chill

STORIES OF GREAT NAMES

which developed into a fever, and on 23 April 1616 he died ; he was buried in Stratford Church on 25 April.

His will had contained clauses which look forward to the ' heirs male ' of Susanna and Judith. There were to be none. No direct descendant of Shakespeare exists. Elizabeth, Susanna's daughter, died without children. Judith had children, but they all died without further issue. One of them, and he the first and a boy, was named Shakespeare after his dead grandfather. Shakespeare Quyny was baptized on 23 November 1616 ; he was buried on 8 May in the following year.

Seven years later, in 1623, Shakespeare's two ' fellows', John Heminge and William Condell, collected and issued the First Folio of the Plays, the most important book to us since the first edition of Dante's *Divine Comedy* in the Middle Ages, and more important even than that *Aeneid* of Virgil which had honoured Augustus Caesar.

VOLTAIRE

One of the more notable of English poets, Robert Browning, towards the end of a poem which dealt with Italy of the seventeenth century, wrote of the Pope whom he used for the poem :—

> 'Tis pity he died unapprised what birth
> His reign may boast of, be remembered by,
> Terrible Pope too of a kind—Voltaire.

The name is familiar enough to those who came in after the eighteenth century, the next to Browning's Pope's. But Voltaire's name has become a myth to many who have little knowledge of him; it has been a war-cry in the intellectual battles of his and the next century. It has stood for freedom and revolt, and though sometimes the rebels have not very well understood the thing they have been fighting, and though the results of the freedom have not been as satisfactory always as could be wished, yet the noble cry of his leadership has been of value to Europe. That cry was *Ecrasez l'infame*—'destroy the infamous thing'. It is to be inquired in what sense he used it and we maintain it.

François Arouet—he added the de Voltaire himself in later life—was a Frenchman, born in Paris on 21 November 1694. His father was a lawyer who transacted the business of several great families. It is worth while to quote what the head of one of them, the Duke of St. Simon, wrote of the son at a later date,

STORIES OF GREAT NAMES

because it shows something of the social relationships in France at that time :—

' Arouet, the son of a lawyer employed by my father and myself, was banished in 1716 for some insolent and satirical verses. I should not write down such a trifle, if this Arouet, having become a poet and a member of the Academy under the name of Voltaire, had not been taken for a personage among literary people, and even gained an apparent importance in certain places.'

The divisions of society in those days were perhaps more marked than before or since. St. Simon despised the middle classes, especially he despised and hated the lawyers, and there were many like him among the dukes and peers of France. François was a lawyer's son—was expected to keep in his place, in which he might be patronized by those who were his superiors in society and inferiors in wit. It was not an impossible position, given goodwill and intelligence. There is nothing to show that Shakespeare objected to being patronized by the Earl of Southampton. Unfortunately, or perhaps fortunately in the end, Voltaire was worse treated than Shakespeare; it was perhaps one of the things that made him an apostle of freedom.

It was at first intended that he also should be a lawyer; when he left school, it was for a law school. But he did not like the career, and though, after a brief trial of diplomacy in the French Embassy at the Hague, he was sent into a lawyer's office, he took the first opportunity to leave it. He had already begun to write verse, and to be known for writing verse; he belonged to a fashionable dining-club; he was on the point of composing a tragedy. Satires of his were

VOLTAIRE

handed about; the great people laughed at them and remembered their author. One of them, the elderly Marquis de Saint-Ange,[1] invited him to leave the lawyer's office and spend a more agreeable time on his own country estate. His father reluctantly assented; the delighted son escaped to leisure, luxury, and the company of nobility. The old Marquis talked of his own part in the court of Louis XIV; Voltaire made notes for his future—his book on the *Age of Louis XIV*. At this suitable moment Louis XIV himself died. The austerity of the Court of his old age, influenced by Madame de Maintenon, his secret wife, a fervently religious woman, died with him, and was succeeded by the gaiety and licence of the Court of his grandson, who was Regent for the infant King, Louis XV. The gay gentlemen filled Paris with satires and libels on the Regent, who, it must be admitted, made a good subject. Voltaire's reputation caused him to be suspected of writing one of the worst of these, and he was sent to the State prison of the Bastille. It was no very arduous imprisonment; he had all he wanted sent in to him; he had brilliant companions, and they all dined every evening with the governor of the prison. Except for the fact that one was not allowed to leave, the Bastille, for such offenders, was a rather gloomy hotel. He was kept there for under a year, and then exiled from Paris for a similar period. Meanwhile he finished his first tragedy, *Oedipe*; it was produced and had an enthusiastic reception. The Regent—an example of the better

[1] Literally translated: 'Holy Angel.' He was an odd angel and had an even less angelic charge to guard.

type of patron—gave him a pension for it. Voltaire, in a letter, thanked his Highness for his income and petitioned him to take no more trouble about his lodging. Such, between two men of intelligence, was the close of the Bastille incident.

He was twenty-two, and famous. He went from manor to manor on visits. He made money; like Shakespeare, he never neglected *that*. He had love-affairs; he had literary quarrels. He could not bear to be criticized with the slightest sharpness, and in such disputes his wit always gave him the advantage. His opponents might be right, but they always found themselves put in the wrong. It was the beginning of his life's warfare, but that war was to grow wider and his central enemy was to be a spiritual sin, and not an intellectual. Already he hated two things—stupidity and cruelty, the two things which in their unholy union were to become *l'infame*—the Infamy.

He opened—it might be said—his first grand attack in the poem he had now finished, called *L'Henriade*, an account and a eulogy of the reign of Henry IV of France. It was a reign his old friend the Marquis de Saint-Ange had much admired; it was a reign in which Voltaire found the greatest example of a thing he even more admired—of tolerance.

Religious tolerance in our days is an accepted virtue; it is one therefore of which the virtuous energy has been lost. Our business to-day is not to lose the thing, but to recover its goodness. We ought to tolerate positively and not negatively, and we ought also—and more often—to regard ourselves as being tolerated by those who disagree with and disapprove of us. But in

VOLTAIRE

Voltaire's day tolerance was not a habit ; it was a new and startling thing, and regarded by the political and ecclesiastical authorities as highly undesirable. All tolerance stops somewhere, and no government ever has been able or (so far as we can see) ever will be able to leave its subjects completely to their own wishes. Whenever a Government regards the safety of the State as being affected, that Government will, and must, ' persecute ' ; that is, take measures to suppress the danger. The Roman government suppressed the early Christians, until, after a period of intellectual change, the Christian idea came to convert and therefore control the Roman world. The governments of the medieval centuries in the same way suppressed those opinions which seemed to them to threaten their stability ; it was the underlying cause of the execution of Joan of Arc. But during the following centuries the basis of government ceased more and more to be metaphysical and became political. It was a mere fact that men could disagree with the general religious views of their nation, and yet remain loyal to their nation. But the old organization and the old laws and the old horrible punishments—worse even than those of our own day—remained in action.

At such a time, when the intellectual energy has changed but the old organization has not changed, the organization tends to be used by the worse types of men. The finer types are content to attack intellect with intellect, and they will suppress disagreement by force only when that disagreement can be shown definitely to threaten the stability of the State. They may be mistaken in their judgement, but they will desire to act on that principle, and their opponents—the new idea, whatever that may be—will be content to show that they do not so threaten that stability. In the time of Voltaire there existed a great intellectual argument about the truth of the Christian religion, and of ideas which had been current for more than a thousand years. This war went on between the best minds on both sides, and it has lasted into our own day. But there was also on the conservative side a very strong mass of conventional opinion which, without being very clear what it held or why it held it, proposed to destroy, as painfully as possible, everything that disagreed with it. There existed, that is to say, a great mass of habitual stupidity combined with habitual cruelty. Such a mass exists at all times; sometimes on one side, sometimes on the other. It has supported Christian and anti-Christian governments, monarchies and republics. Every reformer has to realize that his reform will attract to itself a mass of that kind. It is the effort of all lovers of the intellect and of goodwill to modify, control, or abolish that mass.

That mass, in Voltaire's day, lay behind the King and the Church. It is not to be identified with the King or the Church. The fact that Voltaire's mind was in strong disagreement with the ideas of the Church was a separate fact from his disapproval of the cruel and stupid mass. No doubt to him they sometimes seemed the same. When he wrote 'Destroy the Infamy!' he seems to have applied the phrase to the orthodox religion of his time. But it was not, at bottom, that which his brilliant and sensitive nature hated so much as thick stupidity and gruesome cruelty wherever it appeared;

VOLTAIRE

it is why he attacked bad writers, even of his own intellectual beliefs, more bitterly than good priests of the other side. He spoke always with respect of the Jesuits who had educated him; he satirized Frederick of Prussia who wrote bad verses. No doubt in each case his personal experiences affected his intellectual judgements.

In the *Henriade* then he began to praise the tolerance which Henry IV for political purposes had shown in his reign. He attacked the Infamous Thing and he pretty clearly identified that thing with the clergy and the civil officers who assisted the clergy. What he could not proclaim as a pure gospel he published indirectly as a matter of history in the mode of poetry. But he made the work also a great patriotic epic; it was France in its past splendour which he was celebrating. He succeeded therefore in increasing his reputation; he was taken for the chief of the poets of France of his day. But he was also the most suspect in the eyes of the conservative party and of the infamous mass.

The immediate blow that fell on him soon afterwards had not even the justification of a stupid religious traditionalism; it came from the even less pardonable evil of a silly social insult. He was at the theatre one evening talking to one of the great actresses of the time when a gentleman of one of the noblest houses of France —the Rohans—made a slighting remark about his name. Voltaire took no notice, but a couple of evenings afterwards the nobleman repeated the insult; Voltaire answered sharply: ' My name may not be famous, but at least I know how to honour it.' Rohan touched his sword; the actress went into a diplomatic faint, and the incident closed. A few days later Voltaire was dining with the Duke de Sully, another grand nobleman; in the middle of dinner a message was brought him that he was wanted at the front door. He went down, and was immediately attacked and beaten in the street by De Rohan's footmen, while their master directed them from his coach. Voltaire escaped at last into the house, and begged the Duke de Sully to accompany him to complain to the police. The Duke refused ; the Sullys were not willing to quarrel with the Rohans over a low-born poet, and the noble families were not in the habit of using or approving the officers of the mere civil administration. Voltaire's own protest to the government was ignored. He was angry at being made a subject of pain, insult, and mockery ; he determined to challenge the Rohan. He practised fencing ; he was reported by the secret police to be in a state of wild excitement. He was not by nature a brave man physically ; but he was determined to avenge his reputation. The Rohan family refused to allow so odd a proceeding as that the low-born Voltaire should propose a duel with one of their number. The police who could not be invoked against them were set in action against Voltaire. He was arrested, sent to the Bastille again, and thence sent out of France by his own request. He was furious, and he was determined on revenge. ' I have no sceptre, but I have a pen,' he said, and took ship for England.

It is said that the English always admire the culture of other nations more than their own. But in turn the great men of other nations have sometimes admired the English. It seems almost impossible to us that early

VOLTAIRE

eighteenth century England should be regarded as a home of freedom, but (with certain disadvantages due to its weather and its manners) it was so that Voltaire regarded it. ' Here one can think without fear or flattery ; I am a good mind to stay here in order to learn how to think.' He was puzzled by an English tendency to pretend that they are in fact anything but what they are—poets, philosophers, visionaries. He called on the great dramatist William Congreve ; Congreve paraded himself as a fine gentleman but no writer. ' If you were not a writer I should not have come to see you,' the Frenchman, almost offended, answered. In conversation he admired two English metaphysicians ; his friend said lightly that it was to praise men for playing with air-balloons. Yet he re-published the *Henriade* in England ; everyone admired it and everyone bought it. Voltaire made money. He wrote, in English, a *History of Charles XII* (of Sweden) ; that also was popular. The English admired his wit and his intelligence, and in return he admired their wit, their intelligence, their tolerance, their goodwill. It seemed to him that in England, as compared with France, opinion was free, religion was free, men of letters were free and respected. It is to be remembered always that he was living with and speaking of two classes—high society and the middle-class merchant. There he found the new science—the work and fame of Sir Isaac Newton. Newton's scientific and mathematical work was a revelation to him—' the greatest man that ten centuries have produced'. Sir Isaac had been given a national funeral in Westminster Abbey. England was all that was good and beautiful, but Voltaire was a Frenchman, and even Voltaire desired to live in France. He determined to return to France.

If he had fled in defeat, he returned to conquer. The cause of battle between him and his enemies was fully exposed; that was beyond choice. He was opposed to tyranny—especially stupid tyranny—in the Church, in the State, even in the arts, and certainly to what seemed to him the greatest example of stupid tyranny, war and military force. The field of battle was his own; it was literature in which he was an undoubted master. But he was a master, not only of literature but of a particular kind of literature, a particular kind of attack. Rhetorical outcries, passionate and sincere protests, were no use in France against the Infamy; what was needed was ridicule, and ridicule the more dangerous that it pretended all the time to be simplicity. This is not to say that Voltaire never attacked directly, but it was not his usual habit. He was orthodox, he was respectable—all his arrows sang the same song as they flew, and all of them struck with the same deadly effect in the irritated minds of his orthodox and respectable enemies. For an example—' Faith ', he wrote, ' consists in believing not what seems true but what seems false to our understanding. In saying this, we do not mean at all to allude to the Catholic Faith. We not only respect that Faith, but we possess and profess it.' Yet sometimes he would be devastatingly direct: of the wars of Louis XIV he wrote: ' The people died of hunger to the sound of the Te Deums.' It was always stupidity and cruelty he hated, rather than King or Church;

VOLTAIRE

of the very Church whose ministers he attacked he could write : ' One feels that in everything that Church, when she is free and well-governed, was made to teach the rest.' An English poet, Byron, described him in a stanza.

> The one was fire and fickleness, a child
> Most mutable in wishes, but in mind
> A wit as various,—gay, grave, sage, or wild,—
> Historian, bard, philosopher, combined ;
> He multiplied himself among mankind,
> The Proteus of their talents : But his own
> Breathed most in ridicule,—which, as the wind,
> Blew where it listed, laying all things prone,—
> Now to o'erthrow a fool, and now to shake a throne.

One incident in this period of his life itself expresses the unhypocritical hypocrisy. Voltaire desired to be one of the French Academy. He had written a tragedy; it was presented but regarded with grave suspicion, and the Government compelled it to be withdrawn. Voltaire published it with a dedication to the Pope who was persuaded—we do not know if he read it—to send the author his thanks and blessing. Rome was not France ; it was even more intelligent than France. But in France there was nothing more to be said by the enraged conservatives ; august authority had pronounced the play harmless, whether it knew what it was doing or not. With that assurance Voltaire was victorious. He was elected to the Academy.

Between such triumphs and even more frequent alarms, between flights and concealments on the one hand and receptions and audiences on the other he passed this part of his career. He had many a private quarrel; he who taught tolerance could not conquer his personal angers. Anyone who attacked him—anyone that is who was open to attack—found himself pursued by Voltaire's rage. He was at once generous in spirit and mean in moods. He was often badly treated, and he had no dignity in his personal battles. He would use literature and—less tolerably—the law against his adversaries. Yet an apology or an appeal for mercy would melt him, even in matters of vanity or money. It has been said of him that ' he was never the aggressor, nor was there a good man among his victims.'[1]

He was living at this time with a lady of some standing, a Madame du Chatelet, who was herself a woman of brain and of similar intellectual passions to his own. They worked together; she translated Isaac Newton into French, and confirmed him in his study of mathematics. Their intimacy was enlivened by quarrels over matters of no importance and confirmed by joint ardour for things of great importance. It lasted for sixteen years; when at the end of that time the lady had another lover in view, Voltaire exhibited goodwill; he accepted the situation and the lover, and remained a force in the household.

Another friend also appeared—Frederick, Crown Prince and afterwards King of Prussia. Prussia, under her very able sovereigns, was rising into power among the governments of Europe. This particular sovereign had another aim; he wished to be known through Europe as a really cultured man, a patron of all that

[1] *Voltaire.* H. W. Nevinson. Butterworth.

VOLTAIRE

was latest and greatest in literature. There was no doubt at all who was regarded as the latest and greatest of European men of letters. The State which contained Voltaire was, by that single fact, distinguished; the royal personage who entertained him became, by that supreme guest, a leader of civilization. As once a thousand years before, the barbarian chiefs had desired to bear the titles of Rome—consul or tribune—so now the King of Prussia and the Empress of Russia desired to be called ' enlightened ', ' intellectual ', perhaps even ' poet '. It was a desire limited to abstract discussion and the attitudinizing of the mind; they did not propose as Voltaire would have proposed to purge their governments and illuminate their subjects (outside the Courts) with such lucidities or with the virtue of toleration and free opinion. That was not necessary for their vision of themselves, and perhaps no European nation until the English established schools in India took education seriously in their wider dominions. Certainly Frederick of Prussia did not. But to spread education among his people was not at all the same thing as to be known himself as a friend of M. de Voltaire.

He had written to Voltaire; they exchanged gifts. In 1740 they met. The King laboured to entice Voltaire to Berlin; Madame du Chatelet to keep him in France. The French authorities looked on him with suspicious eyes, yet even they derived satisfaction from the fact that it was a Frenchman who was the idol of foreign rulers (especially as Prussia was then at war with France). They used Voltaire on secret diplomatic errands; the King, on the other hand, arranged

STORIES OF GREAT NAMES

secretly to have certain unpublished and too indiscreet writings of his printed and issued in France, in the hope of compelling him to leave France. But it was not until the death of Madame du Chatelet, ' the half of myself', that he consented. It was 1750 and he was 55 when he moved. In July the King of Prussia received his famous guest in the palace of Potsdam.

A philosopher and a king—a king who was a philosopher and a philosopher who could command a king—for the first weeks a vision of friendship, intellect, and enlightened enjoyment opened before both of them. For the first few weeks Frederick spent money and Voltaire forbore gibes—both unusual events. Paris was half-angry and half-relieved. The attention of the world of culture everywhere was focused on that military and frigid court of Potsdam and Berlin.

But so ideal a life could not last. Each of those two great personages despised the other in his secret heart, and each, in the end, desired only to make the other useful to himself. Voltaire grew bored with revising the King's verses; the King took freedoms with Voltaire which were rather practical jokes than the ease of friendship. He had the walls of Voltaire's lodging painted, in his absence, with apes and peacocks. Voltaire became engaged in a sordid financial law-suit; he could no more bear to lose money gracefully than to bear insolence lightly. Friends repeated their several epigrams. The King had said : ' We squeeze the orange and throw away the peel.' Voltaire had said, of the King's poems : ' Will he never be tired of sending me his dirty linen to wash ? '

Culture has its own wars, and the quarrels of

VOLTAIRE

humanists are no less bitter than those of rulers or priests. There was, at the court of Frederick, another distinguished man, a Frenchman, a scientist, an egotist —but, unfortunately for himself, without both wisdom and its younger sister, wit. His name was Maupertuis. He had a quarrel with a Swiss mathematician, and in the course of it bluntly and scandalously accused his scientific enemy of forging documents. The affair aroused attention in the whole of the international world of European intellect. Voltaire knew both the persons concerned, but he was shocked at the unjust accusation; he wrote an open letter which told the story of the quarrel without discussing it, and was thereby most effective. The King in support of his scientist wrote and published an ineffective reply. Maupertuis published a new book—as learned men do— in which his learning made wild speculations and foolish proposals. Voltaire wrote a squib called *The Diatribe of Dr. Akakia* making exquisite fun of Maupertuis. He read it to the King who, in spite of his kindness for Maupertuis, was delighted by it. But he forbade Voltaire to publish it. Voltaire assented, having already arranged to have it published in the chief cities of Europe; ostensibly by his enemies, if any questions were asked. Maupertuis was furious; the King even more furious. The pamphlet was seized and officially and publicly burnt in Berlin. But all Europe was laughing with Voltaire and at Maupertuis and the King.

Voltaire determined to remain no longer in the patronage of so barbarian a King. He lingered for three months, then he took his leave, on the pretext of visiting a health-resort. The two philosophers parted at Potsdam, coldly.

There was an epilogue, and, years later, another epilogue. Frederick had given Voltaire a private volume of his poems. When, on his slow journey away from Prussia to culture, Voltaire reached Frankfort, a free city outside the Prussian frontiers, he was met and put under arrest by the Prussian minister there, till he should give up the book and various other articles which the King chose to demand. His luggage was following him at a distance, and at Frankfort he was detained until it arrived, and the surrender could be made. Even then he was re-arrested as he left the town, on the belief of the Prussian minister that he must wait for new orders from Frederick. He was taken back to his inn, his money and valuables seized, he himself put under guard, his niece hurried through the town, and insulted by the guard. This state of things lasted for three weeks, until at last explicit orders were received from Frederick. There was no diplomatic, intellectual, or personal excuse for the King. Neither he nor his servants at Frankfort seem to have felt that they needed any. They left future generations to be ashamed on their behalf.

It was Voltaire's last effort to find upon a throne a patron for the enlightenment of society and of the mind. Yet though he never forgave he could be generous, and still, in some odd way, Frederick and he admired and insulted each other. They renewed correspondence years afterwards. When it looked as if Frederick, owing to the results of war, might have to fly from his kingdom, Voltaire wrote offering him a shelter. But

VOLTAIRE

he also went on drawing the pension which the King of Prussia had once given him and had not had the courage or the indecency to withdraw.

It was Voltaire's last approach to a king who desired to be a philosopher. But now he found, as he returned, that he was himself universally recognized as a philosopher who was, intellectually, a king. He bought an estate in Switzerland, but on the borders of France; it was named Ferney and Ferney became the centre of Europe. Its owner was sixty. He took pleasure in posing as an old man. But his energy remained with him, and he appeared through his poses in the prime of his mind. From Ferney he launched upon Europe, one after another his books; those books which, one after another had the same purpose, to oppose the Infamy of cruelty and stupidity, to torment it by mockery, to oppose it by reason, to destroy it by intelligence, tolerance, and goodwill. Part of his method was to describe the fact in the simplest terms, to avoid those phrases which habituate men to their actions till they cannot see their actions. Instead of saying that a man was executed, or that justice was carried out, he would write: 'Four soldiers fired each three bullets into his skull.' Whether this was wise or not is another matter; his concern first was to say *This is what happens*, and second, *Why does it happen?* His statement of the first was always exact; in his answer to the second was the force of his irony, his destructiveness.

It would not do, however, to suppose that Voltaire was nothing but a literary figure, however great. He was not merely that, nor has he been remembered as merely that. The myth of Voltaire is a tradition of intellectual enlightenment, but also of action to maintain and spread such a civilization.

These activities of his were mainly two. The first consisted of his improvements in the village of Ferney himself. It had been a poor collection of hovels when Voltaire bought the estate. He turned his attention to encouraging industries—farming, silk-making, lace-making, watch-making. Certainly the work of that industrial colony had an inestimable advantage over all others; it had one, and only one advertisement—it was the produce of Ferney, of M. de Voltaire. Courts bought it, fine ladies the silk stockings, fine gentlemen the watches. He set the time for Europe—the actual, by his watches; the intellectual, by his books. He achieved a social ideal; but then he had all the necessities—especially a purchasing public. At the same time it must be allowed that he did his best to set up in Ferney a state not only of material but of spiritual success. He did his best to create freedom. What is perhaps the most famous of his books, *Candide*, was published during this period, in 1759. It was, among other things, an attack on an irrational optimism; it struck at all easy views that 'everything is for the best', a view asserted in the book by a certain Dr. Pangloss, whose name has ever stood for that foolish type of placid reassurance. Candide asks 'Why was the world made?' The answer given him, not by Pangloss, is: 'To infuriate us.' In the end, after many adventures, Candide is forced back on a simple maxim: *Cultivez votre jardin,* 'look after your garden'. If Ferney was his garden, Voltaire tried to look after it.

VOLTAIRE

But his other activity, apart from literature, is more famous, and has had a greater effect upon Europe. Voltaire had many pettinesses ; he had an astonishingly sensitive egotism ; he was always tender of himself, both of his safety and his reputation. So are many men, but not many men have also Voltaire's intense passion for justice. It was this which, besides their personal quarrels, had set him at loggerheads with the King of Prussia. It was this which was in 1762 excited by an affair in the great French city of Toulouse. This affair has been known ever since as the Calas case, because the chief victim was named Jean Calas. He was a draper, an old man, and a Protestant in religion. His eldest son committed suicide. By one of those strange and horrible self-creations of rumour, it was reported that in fact he had been murdered by his father for fear he would become a Catholic. The mob of Toulouse believed, and the legal authorities of Toulouse acted on the belief, that this was so. The rest of the Calas family were arrested, imprisoned, tortured, and condemned to death on the most absurd evidence—in fact, upon no evidence. The old man was put to death with the utmost cruelty. The widow, since her husband in his extremest agonies had confessed nothing, had to be acquitted. The other children were confined in convents. One escaped to Switzerland. It was a supreme example of the Infamy in action.

It produced Voltaire in action. The case was reported to him by his friends. He listened, wrote for more information, questioned fugitives, took time to examine and to consider, and was convinced. He then began his campaign. Ferney became the headquarters of the army of justice, and in that army Voltaire enlisted all his friends, all his admirers. The war was not between Protestant and Catholic, not even between believer and unbeliever. It was, purely and simply, between justice and injustice, light and darkness, spiritual honour and spiritual dishonour, righteousness and infamy. Voltaire had nothing at all to gain personally; he gave his time and genius to his plea. He poured out letters ; he stirred up agitations ; he gave money and collected money to give. Wit and mockery were weapons which he did not now use. ' I should be ashamed ', he said, ' if I smiled ' ; and he wrote to a friend concerning another case of intolerance and injustice (they are not the same things) ; ' This is no time for jests ; wit does not go with massacre . . . we ought to seek vengeance . . . is this a time for laughter ? '

Calas was dead, past the prayers or the compensations of men. But his reputation and his family remained. It took the general of the army of salvation three years to win, but he did win. He took care not to endanger his cause by any rashness or exaggeration. Little by little he concentrated his force, not on the horrible creatures at Toulouse, but at Paris and the Court. The King's Council was at last compelled to take action ; the Court of Appeal re-heard the whole case. The dead Calas, and the living members of his house, were declared innocent. The sentence was ordered to be erased from the records of Toulouse. The Infamy had been spectacularly defeated ; the mass of stupidity and cruelty, represented here by the intolerable legal

VOLTAIRE

evil (acting, even so, illegally) had been checked, halted, and defeated upon its own ground.

It was the longest and the fiercest fight, and it is the best known. It has become a symbol and a myth to us. But there were other cases, not less horrible and not less cruel, in which also Voltaire was engaged. Sometimes he won; sometimes he lost. The main thing was that the Infamy was challenged in its own domain and in its own nature by a master whom Europe had acknowledged, and whom none of its power dared touch. Once or twice Voltaire felt some alarm for his own safety; he thought of moving, but he would not leave the Ferney establishment which existed under his authority and encouragement. He was engaged in one of those cases in the last days of his life, and when the news of success reached him he was already dying. He caused a message of congratulation to be sent, ending: ' I see the king is the defender of justice; I shall die happy.' ' Rarely in any age has there lived on this earth a man possessed by this consuming and disinterested passion for justice.'[1]

It was 1778. Voltaire was eighty-four. He desired to see Paris again, and to Paris he determined to go. The doctors warned him against it, but he took no notice of the doctors. He set out on 4 February, and the journey of this old man, still full of energy, still fighting, still a genius and a champion, became a glory. He was a man, and also he was a symbol; crowds thronged to see him, to applaud and almost adore him. Everyone who, in literature, in politics, in religion, had felt the heavy hand of the Infamy, looked on Voltaire

[1] Brailsford. *Voltaire*.

as the great saviour. At one stopping-place young men of rank appeared as waiters to serve M. de Voltaire; at another he was driven by the crush to lock his doors; music was played under his windows; the best horses, the best of everything, must be his. At Paris, when the carriage was stopped at the Customs, he said, laughing: 'I am the only piece of contraband.' The guard recognized him: 'By God, it is M. de Voltaire!' The carriage rolled on; Voltaire, the hero of the world of intellectual honour, had come to the capital of his world.

In Paris the glory continued. Everyone, except the King, the ecclesiastics, and the extreme conservatives, were at his feet and on their knees. The American, Benjamin Franklin, brought his small grandson; Voltaire laid his hand on the child's head, saying: 'God and Liberty.' The Academy sent a deputation. The English ambassador called. Ladies and statesmen thronged to him; crowds ran to see him when he drove out. His last play was performed at the theatre, and on 30 March he went to see it, after paying a state visit to the Academy in the afternoon. There he was put in the President's seat, and congratulated and complimented. He came out to his carriage; an enormous multitude roared round him: 'Voltaire! long live Voltaire!' At the theatre the supreme outbreak of honour reached its climax. When he entered the whole audience rose, shouting, cheering, crying 'Voltaire! Voltaire!' Deafened and overwhelmed he was brought to the front of his box; they crowned him with laurel; he put it aside; a prince lifted it and again set it upon his head. At the end of the play which was presented

VOLTAIRE

through the continuing applause, a bust of Voltaire was set on the stage; the company gathered round it. M. de Voltaire stood in his box; there was but he, for all the rest was only a voice crying his name. He left the theatre; he entered his carriage. Through the multitude it began to move. 'Voltaire!' There was one woman, at least, who did not know the reason of the tumult; she said to another: 'Who is this?' The other answered: 'It is Voltaire, who saved the family of Calas.'

In the midst of this glory, he proposed for himself and for the Academy a new effort. An official Dictionary of the French language was to be prepared; all must take part; he would make himself responsible for the letter A. The doctors begged him to return to Ferney; he replied by sitting up all night to prepare a Memorandum on the Dictionary. That last effort broke him; he fell into a fever, and then into delirium. His mind, that had been so accurate, lost its bearings. Only sometimes he recovered himself; he heard of the case he had helped to win, and dictated his satisfaction. He signed a declaration of orthodoxy, without which he could not hope to be decently buried. It was a weakness and a falsity, but his victories and his proper fame overcome it. He had earlier signed his true declaration of faith: 'I die adoring God, helping my friends, not hating my enemies, detesting superstition— 28 February 1778. Voltaire.'

He died, in charity with all men of charity, in alliance with all desire for lucidity, in love of justice and goodwill, on 30 May 1778. Thirteen years later, in July 1791, his bones were brought in procession from the church vault where they had been hastily buried for fear of the prohibition of the Church, through revolutionary Paris. The daughters of Calas accompanied the bier, on which was inscribed :

' He avenged Calas, La Barre, Sirven, and Montbailly. Poet, philosopher, historian, he gave a great impulse to the human mind ; he made us ready to be free.'

We are not yet free ; we are too much the slaves of our own thoughts and sensations ; prejudice and hate and pride rule us still, as they sometimes ruled Voltaire. But he did not live in vain; the Infamy has never been quite the same since he worked. It was a just impulse that made that woman in the crowd cry on the day of his triumph, not ' It is the friend of the King of Prussia ' or ' It is the great Frenchman ' or ' It is the writer of *Candide* ' or ' It is a poet ', but ' It is Voltaire, who saved the family of Calas.'

JOHN WESLEY

VOLTAIRE was about eight and a half years old when, on 17 June 1703, John Wesley was born in an English vicarage. The life of Voltaire was among courtiers and intellectuals ; his purpose was lucidity and peace ; his means were reason and wit. The life of Wesley was among the poor and the worldly ; his purpose was salvation ; his means were reason and terror. He is a voice crying in the wilderness of the heart; Voltaire a vitriolic whisper in the garden of the mind. Wesley too had his Infamy, but it was all unconverted mankind; nor did he wish to overwhelm but only to change it.

He is a preacher of salvation, but in that eighteenth century to which he and Voltaire belonged he is something more—he is a preacher to crowds. Earlier than the Revolution in France, one hears behind Wesley the movement of the people ; the people, not political, not (for all he taught them) religious, but merely the people. The tale of Wesley lies between those two great powers —God and the people. He desired to unite them. He succeeded and he failed ; in the end, against his intention, he discovered himself to be founding the Methodist Church.

It has been said of him that he 'transformed the English country side ' ; another great religious teacher, William Law, told him in his youth, that he ' wanted to convert the world '. He was born, certainly, in the midst of the one and the results of his work have gone over the other. He is, in fact, in some ways, the

STORIES OF GREAT NAMES

genesis of all modern enthusiastic religion in England and the English dominions, for all that came after him came in a world that he had conditioned. The Church he unintentionally left recovered vigour from him, and those who disagreed, and disagree, most with his methods of proclaiming his doctrine acknowledge most fully the energy of his spirit.

But even this perhaps does not sufficiently summarize the results of his work, for it had a social as well as religious side. The poor in the eighteenth century, more, it might be held, than at any other period of history since the Church had seized Europe, were not only poor but separate, and the division between the governing class and the servile class was more marked than ever before or since. They were two classes, two nations, almost two kinds of beings. Medieval society had been a hierarchy, but a hierarchy which contained a great principle of equality—that every man was in need of salvation. At the time of the Renascence this principle, though it was still theoretically accepted, lost a good deal of ground; it was forgotten or neglected. By the eighteenth century it had lost more —not only in England. But the social effects were perhaps worse in England, where the religious quarrels did not lead to such horrors as the Calas case in France. The Church in England (that is, by this time, the Church of England) still maintained in dogma, and made efforts to maintain in practice, the spiritual equality of man. But the ruling class in England were in general no longer Christian, even formally; and even the Church was affected by the worldliness, coldness, pride, and luxury of the day. The lower classes of

JOHN WESLEY

society were regarded as barbarian, if not merely animal, and were left to their barbarianism. It was largely due to Wesley that the idea of spiritual equality returned; he did not preach it as such, but he treated all men as in need of salvation. The great religious movements which, directly or indirectly, derived from him had many faults and limitations. But as they renewed or assisted spiritual energy, so they helped to restore a social unity; and the slow fight for social justice which makes even our political battles more human than that dreadful separation; the change which has necessitated the use by all parties of humane catchwords, even if they are only catchwords; the moral alteration which has touched indifference with guilt, and hate with humanity; all this has been partly due in England to the work of Wesley and of men like Wesley. It is a result of which he himself, with his passion for religious conversion, might not have thought very much; but the world—both this and the supernatural other—are wider than Wesley. In France they had the Revolution; in England they had the Methodist Revival. But to some extent the result was the same.

Wesley was born in Epworth, a village in Lincolnshire, the son of the parish priest. He had nine brothers and sisters; only one of them, a younger brother, Charles, was to be his companion in the future. His mind was formed in terms of religion; he was brought up to be a Christian, a Churchman, and perhaps a priest. His home was strict, but not unhappy; it was also disturbed by a *poltergeist*, a spirit which made its presence known by noises. It threw things about, clattered bottles, caused knocks to sound in the house, and occasionally pushed against the inhabitants. It was referred to by the family as 'Old Jeffery', and owing to the distinguished career of one of the children who heard it, it has become one of the most famous *poltergeists* on record. The evidence is clear enough to establish the facts though of course *poltergeists* may be denied by the dogmas of materialism.

From his father, his strong-minded mother, and Old Jeffery, Wesley went up to Oxford. His mind and spirit both by nature and by education, were beginning to be immensely concerned with religion and the state of his soul. He was acutely aware of his faults—or those of his faults which he recognized, though they seem to us small enough. He was not good at getting up in the mornings; he liked 'gay company' and 'idle reading' (such as *Robinson Crusoe*); he argued with too much heat—in fact, he took an undue pleasure in all sorts of harmless activities and (so far as lying in bed went) inactivities, and it made him unhappy, though not unhappy enough to give them up. He also liked being praised. He was aware, in short, that there was altogether too much of John Wesley's personal likes and dislikes in John Wesley's world, and he characterized all this as 'known sin'. He was not so wrong, from any religious point of view, as the comfortable ease of most religious persons might suggest. But the activities themselves were harmless enough; it was the desire for something other than they which gave them such dark colours.

At Oxford, however, things became a little better; he found an opportunity of discipline, though not till 1730. By then he was a priest, a Fellow of Lincoln College, a

JOHN WESLEY

lecturer in Greek, and all at twenty-seven. Charles Wesley had come up as an undergraduate in 1728, and John had rebuked him for levity, to which Charles had replied by asking whether his brother expected him to become a saint all at once. But soon Charles had been quickened to join with a few other undergraduates in living a strict religious life, in studying the Bible, in attending church with regularity and devotion, and when John heard of it he hastened to associate himself with them. The group were called by others Bible-moths, the Holy Club, or the Methodists—in allusion to their living by rule. Another member of the group, of future importance in Wesley's life, was George Whitefield, born in 1714, the son of an innkeeper at Gloucester. They began to visit the prisons and the sick, to converse and preach upon religion; it was their duty, and the need of others, though the others did not always understand their need.

Discipline and methodical piety did not altogether satisfy John; he, too, had a need which he did not understand. He talked to William Law, a great man, a writer, and a priest, who put the thing very shortly. He said 'Religion is the most plain, simple thing in the world. It is only *we love Him because He first loved us*'; and again 'Sir, I perceive you would fain convert the world, but you must wait God's own time.' It was true; Wesley desired to be of use to men, to call them to salvation. But he could not honestly say that he knew what this salvation was, or this love of God, and it was not in his nature to be content with belief and morality. He desired more; he desired the experience of a new life. How was he to get it?

STORIES OF GREAT NAMES

The Church in which he was ordained, following the tradition of Christendom, has always looked doubtfully upon demands for such conscious experience; she has demanded of her children a will to believe, to pray, and to act properly, and encouraged them to leave their emotions to look after themselves. But there are always exceptions to this healthy rule. The clergy of the period, however, doing their duty as best they could, found Wesley's insistence on something more than a rule tiresome. He began to be known as a fanatic and a precisian. ' God deliver me ', he said, ' from a half-Christian.' But it was widely felt that John Wesley considered most Christians of his acquaintance as half-Christians.

In 1735 he had an opportunity of going, with his brother Charles, to America. General Oglethorpe, the founder of the colony of Georgia, wished to take there a few proper persons to preach religion. Charles was going as his secretary. John determined to go also; he thought that missionary work among the Red Indians might produce better results than it seemed to do at home. On the ship with him were certain of the Moravian Brethren, a German religious body. The ship being once caught in a storm Wesley observed the Moravians calmly singing. He asked one of them afterwards : ' But were you not afraid ? ' ' I thank God I am not afraid to die.' ' But your women ? your children ? ' ' Our women and children are not afraid to die.' To die meant to Wesley to be flung into the judgement of God, and he knew he was still very much afraid to fall into the judgement. The new life, in which there was no such fear, shone before him, still

JOHN WESLEY

unachieved. His sense of this was confirmed by further conversations with the Moravians. He was asked whether he knew that he was in a state of salvation; he hesitated and spoke of hope; the Moravian asked: ' Do you *know* ? ' and though Wesley brought himself to say ' I do ', he felt he was using empty words.

In America he got no farther. He had, on the whole, a difficult time with the colonists; he had a more difficult time through a lady with whom he fell in love, and who seemed willing enough to marry him. But he did not know if he ought to marry; the Moravians advised against it; his uncertainties worried the girl, and eventually she married someone else. Then he grew disturbed about her spiritual life; he thought she was falling away; he took steps to rebuke her. There was a public uproar; eventually he slipped away and after a dangerous journey through the forest, took ship for home. The old life had agonized him, but the new was still hidden. He examined himself continuously, and came to the conclusion that he was still deep in unbelief, pride, and levity of spirit. ' Oh, who shall convert me ? I have a fair summer religion . . . I have learned, in the ends of the earth, that my whole heart is altogether corrupt and abominable.' He had believed it before, but it is likely that his emotional experiences in Georgia had made it very real to him. The heart that, for whatever reason, loses the beloved object, is apt to look on itself as abominable; it translates—a dangerous habit—its failure into itself.

But he knew at least that his heart was not unique; other men's hearts were as corrupt, and his passion of repudiation broke out in the pulpit. When he was back in London he sometimes preached in churches where he was invited. It often happened that he was afterwards warned that he would not be invited, or indeed allowed, to preach there again. The energy even of the unconverted Wesley was too much for the quiet of the Church. The Moravians whom he got to know at home told him that he had not faith, but that if he preached faith he would reach faith. He obeyed; he urged himself on; he clamoured for faith, for the new life, in pulpits, on the roads, in prisons, to all sorts and conditions of men. His heart, abominable as it might be, throbbed and ached with desire.

Charles, who had returned from America before his brother, had been ill of pleurisy, and was in the same spiritual state as his brother; he also had been warned by their Moravian friend that he had no faith. Perhaps, as sometimes happens, his physical illness quickened his spiritual life; at all events John heard that he had found ' rest to his soul '. The crisis had been relieved in him; the sense of the new life had come. John was more agonized than ever; the sense of his own futility and iniquity—the sense, in fact, of *himself*—rose in him; he said he was ' sold under sin '. It was Wednesday, 24 December 1738; Voltaire was at Cirey, with Madame du Chatelet, studying Newton, and composing satire against the Infamy.

On the evening of that day Wesley went to a meeting of a group of religious friends in Aldersgate Street, in the City of London. One of them read aloud from the preface by Martin Luther to the Epistle of Saint Paul to the Romans. Wesley was listening. He wrote

JOHN WESLEY

later: 'About a quarter before nine, while he was describing the change which God works in the heart through faith in Christ, I felt my heart strangely warmed; I felt I did trust in Christ, Christ alone, for salvation: and an assurance was given me, that he had taken away *my* sins, even *mine*, and saved *me* from the law of sin and death.'

The great, the desired, assurance had been given; the new life had begun. It was not placid; when he went home he found himself still subject to inward temptations and distresses. But he defined the difference himself: ' And herein I found the difference between this and my former state chiefly consisted. I was striving, yea, fighting, with all my might under the law, as well as under grace: but then I was sometimes, if not often, conquered; now I was always conqueror.'

It is the well-known alteration of the spirit, repeated in many of the spiritual masters. Newman (to quote only one other example) found the same thing in the next century; after his submission to the Church of Rome he was troubled but never doubtful. It may be a yielding of this or that kind, to or from this or that idea, involving this or that dogma; that is all secondary. The primary element is the sudden rooting of the soul in a profound *otherness*, the otherness which Wesley called God. He knew his salvation.

It has to be remembered, however, that such an experience brings with it a natural, but unwise, corollary, which Wesley did not escape. He tended to think that some such experience was a necessity for every man who was sincere in his religion. He

STORIES OF GREAT NAMES

demanded it, for he believed it the only safe foundation. It was this demand which helped, slowly but surely, to set so great a missionary at odds with his Church, the Church of England. For that Church, like the Church of Rome and the Churches of the East, has only demanded (as was said before) right belief and good intention; and the Church of England in the eighteenth century was even more doubtful about these experiences than at other times. It thought the demand for them, the waiting upon them, 'fanatical', as to Wesley the bishops and priests and laity who had never consciously undergone that conviction seemed to be cold and dead, unchristian, poor idols in the true world of the living God.

John indeed found that while his brother Charles went with him on the way, another brother, Samuel, also a priest, was very mistrustful of such roads. They would ' do a world of mischief ', he said of his brothers, and of John: ' I know not where to direct him, or where he is—I pray God to stop the progress of this lunacy.' Samuel was a good man, but what he called bitterly ' indwellings and experiences ' were not for him.

But John was contented; he was—in a long paper he proved to his mind what he had experienced in his heart—' a new creature '. He had seven reasons for it, all supported by texts with which he found his own knowledge of himself agreed. His only sense of failing was that he had no *joy*; he did not *love* God; he was not sufficiently moved or exalted; therefore he was not ' in the full and proper sense of the words ' a new creature, but he humbly trusted that that would come.

JOHN WESLEY

He paid a short visit to the Moravians in Germany. He did not quite approve of their methods, and they did not quite approve of his spiritual state. The children of the second birth had their own difficulties and their own disputes.

But, however much he might still desire to improve, he had now a foundation from which to act. ' Give me standing room ', said Archimides, ' and I will move the world.' John Wesley had found spiritual standing room in his awareness of and reconciliation with that sense of salvation and power ; on his return to London he proceeded to move the world. He had interviews with two bishops, who, while not exactly disapproving of experience, discouraged the demand for it, and suggested prudence. ' God deliver me from what the world calls Christian prudence,' said Wesley, and entered upon his career of preaching and exhorting. There were by this time a number of local societies of Methodists, some with knowledge of salvation, some without. John and Charles, and their friend George Whitefield, with some others, began to labour among them ; they preached, in such churches as were opened to them, to wider congregations ; where they went they were accompanied by conversions, some quiet, some exalted, excited and exciting. There was a meeting in 1739 where, under the stress of emotion, ' many cried out for exceeding joy, and many fell to the ground '. He visited asylums, and the lunatics were subdued before him. The mad received peace, and the sane ecstasy.

It was, however, Whitefield who was responsible for the opening of a wider door, a door out of the walled rooms and churches in which hitherto the great movement had existed, a door on to the fields and open spaces. At Bristol, on Saturday, 17 February 1739, he stood upon a little rise in the ground and began under the open sky to address the miners of the district. He repeated his innovation; 'the trees and hedges were full . . . the fire is kindled in the country.' The open fields of Bristol were as convenient for his gospel as the closed chambers of London; his power shook his hearers to outcries and tears, to repentance and conversion. In some cases this was followed by relapse, but in many it remained firm. The field-preaching of Whitefield declared and demanded the deepest equality of men.

Whitefield had to leave Bristol; he sent for Wesley, and when he came urged him also to adopt the new method. Wesley at first was uneasy; he had been, as he said, ' all my life tenacious of every point relating to decency and order '. But he remembered that Christ had preached the Sermon ' on the Mount ', and it could not be denied that that was field-preaching; he gave way. On 1 April 1739 he spoke ' from a little eminence to about three thousand people'. His text (he said) was ' *The Spirit of the Lord is upon me, because he hath anointed me to preach the Gospel to the poor. He hath sent me to heal the broken-hearted; to preach deliverance to the captives, and recovery of sight to the blind; to set at liberty them that are bruised; to proclaim the acceptable year of the Lord.*'

The date of Wesley's conversion was the birthday of his own salvation, but this other date is the beginning of the great revival in its fullness. The equality and unity of men, their general guilt, their common need,

JOHN WESLEY

the possibility of their universal, and yet individual, salvation was proclaimed by a voice which shook their hearts and overthrew their emotion and convinced them of their sin and offered them a known, an experienced, a perfect, redemption. One after another was ' overwhelmed with joy and love '. He saw, and he saw rightly and exactly, many all round him becoming new creatures. He wrote to his brother Samuel : ' I have seen (as far as it can be seen) many persons changed in a moment from the spirit of horror, fear, and despair, to the spirit of hope, joy and peace ; and from sinful desires, till then reigning over them, to a pure desire of doing the will of God. These are matters of fact, whereof I have been, and almost daily am, an eye or ear witness. Upon the same evidence (as to the suddenness and reality of change) I believe, or know this, touching visions and dreams : I know several persons in whom this great change from the power of Satan unto God, was wrought either in sleep, or during a strong representation to the eye of their minds of Christ, either on the cross, or in glory. This is the fact : let any judge of it as they please. But that such a change was then wrought appears, not from their shedding tears only, or sighing, or singing psalms, but from the whole tenour of their life, till then in many ways wicked, from that time holy, just, and good.'

The violence of the manifestations is not to be confused with the reality of the change. Charles Wesley always,[1] and John in later life, distrusted such

---

[1] He told one woman, who was breaking into cries and convulsions, that they gave him no better opinion of her, and she stopped. He ordered another to be carried out, and she walked away.

violence—the cryings and the convulsions, the fallings and the foamings, the delirious paraphernalia of change. But to deny change because of its delirious exhibition is as foolish as to make delirious exhibition a part of change. What is certain is that John Wesley all his life had a particular power on others ; and the cause of it may be simply that he loved them. He had in him a direct energy of love ; it struck, it troubled, it agonized them, but as often it soothed and consoled and refreshed them. Charles was more intellectual ; Whitefield was a greater orator ; both were as sincere in their devotion to God and their work. But perhaps neither of them had so direct and intense a love of those they met. They desired the salvation of their hearers for a score of good and holy reasons, but Wesley desired it merely because his hearers were men and women ; he loved them, and wished them to be happy in their new creation. So, for fifty-three years, he went about England, and transformed men and English life, and nothing was ever the same again.

He had, of course, opposition, and he had his own personal difficulties. The first was double—from opponents within the Societies, and from opponents without. Hostility within again was double ; there were doctrinal disputes, and there were ' false brethren'. He was compelled to disagree and separate from the Moravians on one point of teaching, from Whitefield on another, and on a third he very nearly came to a division with Charles. Such disputes were inevitable, and the separations were inevitable when neither side was prepared to be convinced by the other or to accept any of the historic decisions of the whole Church.

JOHN WESLEY

When it came to the last resort John Wesley had no idea of allowing any decision but his own to dominate the Societies; once, when his lay-preachers were disagreeing with him, he made it clear that he was the master. It was, he said, a fundamental rule in Methodism that the preachers should act '*when* and *where* I appoint'. He might have added *as* and *how* and any other adverb; all that was implicit in the situation and in his mind. He would be master, but it is true that if Methodism was to be saved from anarchy he had to be master, and when it came to the point he saw to it that he was.

He declared: 'Neither did I, at any of those times, divest myself of any part of that power which the providence of God had cast upon me, without any design or choice of mine. What is that power? It is a power admitting into, and excluding from, the Societies under my care; of choosing and removing stewards; of receiving, or not receiving, helpers; of appointing them when, where, and how to help me; and of desiring any of them to meet me, when I see good. And as it was merely in obedience to the providence of God, and for the good of the people, that I at first accepted this power, which I never sought; nay, a hundred times laboured to throw off; so it is on the same considerations, not for profit, honour, or pleasure, that I use it at this day.'

There were some who shocked and betrayed him— betrayed him in the sense of going against the very ideas of his life while pretending submission. He had sometimes to excommunicate. But such things were rare, considering the swift growth of the Societies; one of the blessed things about the whole movement is its sincerity, virtue, and peace in itself. It needed that, for it did not find peace without. Hardly less astonishing than the peace within the Societies is the opposition that they, but especially Wesley's preaching, aroused in the world. The ecclesiastical authorities had discouraged the new evangelical fervour from the beginning; if they were wrong, at least they were wrong with an excuse. With this there was mingled the inevitable objection which parish priests felt to the setting up in their parishes of societies based on experiences provoked by travelling preachers and owning a kind of allegiance to a head outside the usual ecclesiastical administration. Selfish and unselfish reasons combined to close the churches to Wesley, to raise against him the hostility of the clergy, and to provoke it also against the societies now forming a connexion all through England. The members of those societies were in some cases responsible. Some of them, regarding their own experiences as the only means of salvation, talked of their old fellow-Christians as being dead in darkness and sin. They may sometimes have been right, but it did not make for peace.

It was not, however, the authorities of the Church only who harried the new apostle. The mob, that great embodiment of the lowest emotions, mocked him and often attacked him. He could control and convert them when he spoke, but they would not let him speak. The mere pleasure in hunting and hurting broke out around him; crowds would carry him to a magistrate—not that they wished to apply the law, but that it gave

JOHN WESLEY

them brutal amusement. It seemed sometimes as if Wesley, and for that matter his companions and followers also, were in danger of losing life. The mob was sometimes incited or encouraged by gentlemen of higher rank. People of fashion, with few exceptions, no more cared for Wesley than the ranks of the imperial Court of Rome had cared for St. Paul or St. Peter. Horace Walpole, a typical gentleman of his age, despised him; Beau Nash, the Master of Ceremonies at the society resort of Bath, had a not very successful interview with him. 'Nash affirmed that he was acting contrary to the laws. " Besides," said he, " preaching frightens people out of their wits." " Sir," replied Wesley, " did you ever hear me preach ? " " No," said the Master of Ceremonies. " How then can you judge of what you never heard ? " Nash made answer, " By common report." " Sir," said Wesley, " is not your name Nash ? I dare not judge of you by common report : I think it not enough to judge by." When Nash desired to know what the people came there for, one of the congregation cried out, " Let an old woman answer him : You, Mr. Nash, take care of your body, we take care of our souls, and for the food of our souls we come here." He found himself a very different person in the meeting-house from what he was in the Pump-room or the assembly, and thought it best to withdraw.'[1]

On the whole, however, the disturbances died away. The magistrates suppressed the riots ; the mob grew tired of its amusements ; the Methodists sustained their vocation.

[1] Southey. *Life of Wesley.*

STORIES OF GREAT NAMES

But so satisfactory a defeat did not always take place. Both Wesley and the other preachers suffered actual insolence from the mob. On one occasion, after a free fight between two crowds, he found himself, late on a rainy night, in the hands of a hostile mob, who were pouring down a steep hill. The classic description of the scare is in Southey's *Life of Wesley*, and cannot be bettered. ' The entrance to the town was down a steep hill, and the path was slippery, because of the rain. Some of the ruffians endeavoured to throw him down ; and if they had accomplished their purpose, it was not likely that he would ever have risen again ; but he kept his feet. Part of his clothes was torn off ; blows were aimed at him with a bludgeon, which, had they taken effect, would have fractured his skull ; and one cowardly villain gave him a blow on the mouth which made the blood gush out. With such outrages they dragged him into the town. Seeing the door of a large house open, he attempted to go in, but was caught by the hair, and pulled toward the end of the main street, and there he made toward a shop-door, which was half open, and would have gone in, but the shop-keeper would not let him, saying, that, if he did, they would pull the house down to the ground. He made a stand, however, at the door, and asked if they would hear him speak ? Many cried out, " No, no ! Knock his brains out ! Down with him ! Kill him at once ! " . . . He obtained a hearing, and began by asking, " What evil have I done ? Which of you have I wronged, in word or deed ? " His powerful and persuasive voice, his ready utterance, and his perfect self-command, stood him on this perilous emergency in

JOHN WESLEY

good stead. A cry was raised, "Bring him away! Bring him away!" When it ceased, he then broke out into prayer; and the very man who had just before headed the rabble, turned and said, "Sir, I will spend my life for you! Follow me, and not one soul here shall touch a hair of your head!" The man had been a prize-fighter at a bear-garden: his declaration therefore carried authority with it; and when one man declares himself on the right side, others will second him, who might have wanted courage to take the lead. A feeling in Wesley's favour was now manifested, and the shopkeeper, who happened to be the mayor of the town, ventured to cry out, "For shame! for shame! Let him go"; having, perhaps, some sense of humanity and of shame for his own conduct. The man who took his part conducted him through the mob, and brought him, about ten o'clock, back to Wednesbury in safety, with no other injury than some slight bruises. The populace seemed to have spent their fury in this explosion; and when, on the following morning, he rode through the town on his departure, some kindness was expressed by all whom he met. A few days afterwards, the very magistrates who had refused to see him when he was in the hands of the rabble, issued a curious warrant, commanding diligent search to be made after certain "disorderly persons, styling themselves Methodist preachers, who were going about raising routs and riots, to the great damage of His Majesty's liege people, and against the peace of our Sovereign Lord the King."'

There was on the other hand some danger of the Methodists being regarded as supporters of the exiled royal family, the Stuarts. There had been a rising in favour of the Old Pretender, as he was called, in 1715; and his son Charles Edward was to lead another in 1745. In 1744 the authorities were in a considerable state of nerves, and ready to construe any phrase as seditious. It is a disease from which governments always suffer—none the less because sometimes they are quite right, and the phrases are seditious. It was the habit of the Jacobites in England to drink the health of the King over the water; there were songs and sayings about 'a return'. In Yorkshire an enthusiastic loyalist heard Charles Wesley speaking of the time when the Lord would call home his banished ones. He supposed the Stuarts to be meant, whereas in fact it was all mankind—'those' as Charles explained to the magistrate before whom he was brought, 'who confess themselves strangers and pilgrims upon earth'. They believed him and let him go.

But slowly the perseverance of the Methodists prevailed. The mob grew tired of their amusements; more and more of the magistrates grew anxious to suppress the real rioters. The Societies were enabled to work in peace. It is to be remembered that up to a late period in Wesley's career there was no thought of separation from the Church of England; in fact, it would be true to say that he never did intend to separate from the Church of England. The separation, and the founding of one of the greatest of the Free Church bodies, came about, inevitably, as a result of the view which the clergy took of the Methodists and the Methodists of the clergy. They regarded each other respectively as dangerous enthusiasts and as dying

JOHN WESLEY

souls. Besides which, the Methodist organization grew more complex year by year.

Into this separation, already in progress before Wesley died, it is hardly possible to go here, for it turned on special questions—the highly theological problems of Holy Orders and the Sacraments of the Church. Charles saw the division coming; it was grief and pain to him. John refused to contemplate it, yet his actions in declaring himself capable of ordaining priests—a power reserved to bishops in the Church of England— inevitably determined it.

Wesley began it by appointing certain other preachers to assist him. He drew up a number of rules for them. Some were good, and ordinary, enough : ' Be diligent. Be serious. Believe evil of no-one. Speak evil of no-one. Be punctual.' One or two were more doubtful though perhaps necessary in the circumstances. ' Take no step towards marriage without first acquainting us with your design. Tell every one what you think wrong in him, and that plainly, and as soon as may be, else it will fester in your heart. Make all haste to cast the fire out of your bosom.' One or two were noble. ' Be ashamed of nothing but sin ; not of fetching wood (if time permit) or of drawing water ; not of cleaning your own shoes, or your neighbour's. You have nothing to do but to save souls. Therefore spend and be spent in this work. And go always, not only to those who want you, but to those who want you most.'

The preachers were not to engage in trade ; they were not to print anything without Wesley's consent ; they were not to sell ' pills, drops, balsams, or medicines '. They were to rise early and preach early.

STORIES OF GREAT NAMES

They were not to touch alcohol or take snuff; they were—it is a sublime phrase—to deny themselves ' every useless pleasure of sense, imagination, honour '. By the scope of that definition the new life, arising from the new birth, is shown ; all ordinary values were overturned, and nothing but the kingdom of God was to ordain the desires of those converted souls.

To encourage this new doctrine there were to be meetings of the various societies once a week, when open confession was to be made by all of all sin committed or imagined since the last meeting. It was a habit which had been attempted, it seems, by the early Christians, and had had to be abandoned by the Church in general. The monastic bodies still retained it, but for the poor in spirit it was too hard and too dangerous a way. The great peril of the Methodists was the same as possesses all religious bodies founded on *experience* as distinguished from dogma : that a state of things only tolerable to saints and disciplined students should be demanded from ' babes in grace '.

Presently chapels began to be built and schools to be formed. Wesley, though he did not encourage ' vain learning ' in his preachers, believed in the education of the young. Unfortunately for the young he also believed in their conversion, and in some places the most shocking scenes took place, when children of five or under were encouraged to expect and consciously experience the direct visitation of God. Christ in his own dealings with children does not seem to have agitated them as Wesley thought it necessary to do. Yet all these things were, so to speak, by accident, and none of them must hide from us the picture of the man,

JOHN WESLEY

growing old, continuously travelling, continuously preaching, continuously praying, riding from village to village and town to town, with one word for lords and farmers, labourers and women, for all classes and all vocations, converting the world at last, so far as his strength would carry him, and converting it in as pure a love as is, with rare exceptions, given to man. ' If we die without love ', he wrote, ' what will knowledge avail ? . . . Love the Lord . . . love your neighbour . . . I am sick of opinions . . . give me a man laying himself out in the world of faith, the patience of hope, the balance of love.'

The work was not confined to England. It spread to Wales, to Scotland, to Ireland. In Wales the difficulty of language hampered its progress, though (as Wesley himself saw) the Welsh were peculiarly likely to be moved by the clarion of salvation he desired to blow. In Scotland there was a different and less reasonable, difficulty. The Scotch were already theologians, and theologians of an austere kind. They were rooted in their doctrines. ' The hand of the Lord ', said Wesley, ' was almost entirely stayed in Scotland.' He did not quite understand it, and he, naturally, was inclined to blame his hearers. It is ' a people ', he said at Glasgow, ' who *hear* much, *know* everything, and *feel* nothing '. But he was not quite correct. The Scotch people had absorbed into their minds, almost into their bodies, the austere theology of John Calvin, and they were already organized into an austere, but living, Church. The Church of England, at its best of discipline, was lax compared with them, and Wesley's voice and gospel could find entrance to many hearts. But against the stern race that lay on the other side of the ancient Roman walls, he beat more or less in vain. He was not even attacked. He was defeated, and defeated by the only thing that could defeat him, a religion as passionate and even more stern than his own. The same thing happened to a large extent in Ireland. The doctrine of the Roman Church opposed as firm a wall as that of Calvin, though in the Protestant part of the country he made headway, and towards the end of his life he had a great personal popularity.

In 1766 he was begged to go over into America and help there. Things were very bad, according to the more earnest Christians. People 'are drinking their wine in bowls, and are jumping and dancing, and serving the Devil, in the groves, and under the green trees'. Wesley did what he could; preachers were allowed to volunteer to go. But the spread of the Methodists at the time was hindered by the outbreak of the American Revolution. Wesley had no use at all for the people as rulers—he who had such a passionate belief in the unique value of every individual soul, and in the equality of all souls. ' There is most liberty of all, civil and religious, under a limited monarchy; there is usually less under an aristocracy; and least of all under a democracy.' That other great Englishman of the same period, Dr. Johnson, agreed with him. It sometimes seems as if the English had achieved a very great share of political and social freedom by the simple process of not believing in it.

It is worth making a pause on Johnson's name to quote once more his famous comment made in

JOHN WESLEY

Mrs. Thrale's house at Streatham, during breakfast on Tuesday, 31 March 1778, the year when the headquarters of the Methodists were established in the new chapel at City Road. He said ' John Wesley's conversation is good, but he is never at leisure. He is always obliged to go at a certain hour. This is very disagreeable to a man who loves to fold his legs and have out his talk, as I do.'

In the next year Johnson gave Boswell a letter of introduction to Wesley. Boswell's account is as follows :—

' He had, before I left London, resumed the conversation concerning the appearance of a ghost at Newcastle upon Tyne, which Mr. John Wesley believed, but to which Johnson did not give credit. I was, however, desirous to examine the question closely, and at the same time wished to be made acquainted with Mr. John Wesley ; for though I differed from him in some points, I admired his various talents, and loved his pious zeal. At my request, therefore, Dr. Johnson gave me a letter of introduction to him.

" To the Reverend Mr. John Wesley.

" Sir,—Mr. Boswell, a gentleman who has been long known to me, is desirous of being known to you, and has asked this recommendation, which I give him with great willingness, because I think it very much to be wished that worthy and religious men should be acquainted with each other. I am, Sir, your most humble servant,

" SAM. JOHNSON."

" May 3, 1779."

STORIES OF GREAT NAMES

'Mr. Wesley being in the course of his ministry at Edinburgh, I presented this letter to him, and was very politely received. I begged to have it returned to me, which was accordingly done. His state[ment] of the evidence as to the ghost did not satisfy me.'

In 1751 Wesley married; the marriage was not a success. His wife was determined to command him who commanded the Societies, and he was determined that she should not. He had laid down before the marriage that he would not preach one sermon nor travel one inch the less on account of it, nor did he. But, necessary as that rule may have been to his supernatural duty, it was not calculated to produce a comfortable household. 'Attempt no more to abridge me of my liberty,' he wrote to his wife, not only in relation to journeys and sermons. He expected a submission of her to himself and to a law which even he might have found it difficult fully to obey: 'Of what importance', he asked her, 'is your character to mankind?' She made, however, her temper of importance to him, and the apostle of conversion endured private persecutions as bitter as the public hostility. At last they parted; she died in 1781.

Wesley was then seventy-eight, and had another ten years to live. 'Leisure and I have taken leave of each other,' he had written. 'I propose to be busy as long as I live.' He carried out his intention. Of the causes which contributed to his long life and capacity he reckoned his 'evenness of temper' as among chief; 'I *feel* and *grieve*; but, by the Grace of God, I *fret* at nothing.' Other contributing causes—not perhaps so

JOHN WESLEY

easily emulated by the rest of us—were his generally rising at four and preaching at five, and his never travelling less than 4,500 miles a year. He had one or two illnesses, including an operation, but in 1780 he was as well as in 1740. It was part of the good fortune of the Societies that not only did the first members live under that direct and personal influence, but the second generation also. Children were born into them, and grew up, and had other children, and still Mr. Wesley came riding—or, in his age and under persuasion driven in a carriage—along the English roads, exhorting, encouraging, blessing. His energy was not sapped, nor his control loosened ; his zeal was as fiery and his government as firm as ever. He wrote in 1785, when he was eighty-two, 'It is now eleven years since I have felt any such thing as weariness' ; three years later he admitted a certain loss of agility, but he still repeated that he did not feel 'any such thing as weariness'.

In 1788 his brother died ; in 1789 he himself admitted 'I now find I grow old', in 1790 'it seems nature is exhausted'. That was at the end of June ; on the 17th February next he took cold after preaching at Lambeth, and a fever came on him. It was thirteen years since, also in the late winter, Voltaire had similarly suffered from the mere energy of his labour. Two men more different could hardly be imagined, nor two men more alike. The necessity of spiritual integrity was upon each of them, and the energy of each rose to meet it. Six days after the Lambeth sermon he delivered his last sermon, and on 2 March, a week later, in quiet of body and peace of mind, he died. At the funeral the phrase ' the soul of our dead brother ' was changed to ' the soul of our dead father '. It was fitting ; there were on that day, at home and beyond seas, some hundred and thirty thousand men and women who acknowledged the gospel and practised the discipline of John Wesley.

NOTES

By R. D. BINFIELD

ALEXANDER

PAGE 1.

5. *Plutarch:* famous Greek biographer of the first century A.D. His great work was the *Parallel Lives* of twenty-three Greeks and twenty-three Romans, arranged in pairs.

6. *Julius Caesar:* see pages 29-65.

8. *one of the chief subjects for medieval poetry:* the principal romances concerning him are the great French *Roman d'Alexandre* of the twelfth century, some 20,000 lines, and the English *King Alisaunder* of the thirteenth century, 8,000 verses.

10. *in Shakespeare:* see the Masque of the Worthies—*Love's Labour's Lost*, V. ii.

11. *Dryden wrote a poem on him:* John Dryden (1631-1700). His *Alexander's Feast, or the Power of Music* was an ode in honour of St. Cecilia, the patroness of music.

12. *Flecker:* James Elroy Flecker (1884-1915). The poems were *The Ballad of Iskander* and *Santorin*.

13. *Mr. Robert Graves:* (b. 1895). The poem is *The Clipped Stater*.

PAGE 2.

14. *Socrates:* the great Greek philosopher (469-399 B.C.) whose teaching was immortalized by his pupil Plato.

15. *Sophocles:* Greek tragedian (495-406 B.C.), author of *Oedipus the King, Electra, Antigone*, etc.

25. *Byzantine emperors:* the rulers of the eastern division of the Roman Empire, the capital of which was Constantinople from A.D. 395-1453.

27. *eastern scimitars:* Constantinople was captured by the Turks in 1453.

NOTES

28. *western crusaders:* between A.D. 1096 and 1270, eight crusades were undertaken by the Christian powers to regain Jerusalem and the Holy Land.

32. *its king:* Philip II reigned over Macedon from 359-336 B.C. during which time his wisdom as a politician and his exploits as a general made it a powerful kingdom.

PAGE 3.

6. *Augustus Caesar:* the nephew of Julius Caesar, and Roman emperor.

PAGE 4.

5. *Aristotle. Plato:* as Plato (428-347 B.C.) was the pupil of Socrates, so Aristotle (384-322 B.C.) was the pupil of Plato.

PAGE 6.

1. *Thebes:* the capital of Boeotia in Greece.

14. *Antipater:* (398?-319 B.C.), regent of Macedonia during Alexander's eastern expedition. On the death of Alexander he was left in command.

22. *the Macedonian phalanx:* see page 10.

26. *Diogenes:* this austere philosopher had a large earthenware jar or tub as a dwelling.

PAGE 7.

8. *the oracle of Delphi:* the oracle was situated on the slopes of Mt. Parnassus. The priestess of Apollo, called the Pythia, was supposed to be inspired by the sulphurous vapours issuing from a cavity in the ground, when the oracle was consulted. The answers were usually capable of two interpretations.

24. *Caesar was to cross the Rhine:* see page 42.

PAGE 8.

4. *Demosthenes:* his orations to rouse his countrymen to the danger of Philip of Macedon produced the word 'philippic' for bitter invective.

ALEXANDER

16. *The great Emathian conqueror*: from Milton's sonnet *When the assault was intended to the City*. Emathia was the original seat of the Macedonian monarchy.

PAGE 9.

8. *Darius*: Darius III of Persia, who succeeded on the murder of Arses.

24. *aquiline*: like an eagle, i.e. hook-nosed.

31. *Thracians*: a warlike people from that part of north-east Greece bounded by the Black Sea, the Hellespont, and the Aegean. See map opposite page 1.

PAGE 10.

15. *Priam . . . the King of Troy*: Priam was slain by Neoptolemus, the son of Achilles, after the fall of Troy to the Greeks.

PAGE 11.

7. *the Granicus*: a river in North-west Asia Minor. In this action the Macedonians numbered 30,000 foot and 5,000 horse; the Persians 600,000 foot and 20,000 horse.

PAGE 12.

4. *satraps*: provincial governors in the Persian Empire.

PAGE 13.

3. *Tyre*: see map opposite page 1. Alexander was seven months in taking it.

3. *Gaza*: about 130 miles south of Tyre. Here again a long siege was necessary.

20. *Alexandria*: became the capital of Egypt under the Ptolemies.

22. *intellect and art*: the Alexandrian period of Hellenistic literature existed until the Roman conquest of Greece, 146 B.C.

31. *Jupiter-Ammon*: Jupiter was a Roman deity, and came to be identified with the Greek Zeus. Ammon, the

NOTES

supreme God of the Egyptians in Theban religion was also identified with Zeus.

PAGE 15.

10. *Euphrates* . . . *Tigris:* two rivers flowing into the Persian Gulf. See map opposite page 1.

PAGE 17.

12. *phalanxed infantry:* see page 10.

PAGE 19.

3. *Persepolis:* see map opposite page 1. Ruins of this splendid city still exist. Cf. Marlowe, *Tamburlaine* II, iii, 754.

20. *Herat:* in north-east Afghanistan.

PAGE 21.

3. *Babylon* . . . *Memphis* . . . *Cyrene:* see map opposite page 1. The first of these famous cities was on the river Euphrates; the second was a very ancient city of Egypt; the third was a Greek colony in north-west Africa.

8. *Jascartes:* (or Jaxartes) a river flowing into the Aral Sea.

22. *Heracles:* (or Hercules) the son of Zeus and Alcmena, a valiant hero of many legends who obtained divine honours after his death.

22. *Castor and Pollux:* twin son of Zeus, known as the Dioscuri, and friends of navigators.

PAGE 22.

15. *Euripides:* (480-406 B.C.), the youngest and most modern-minded of the three Athenian tragedians.

PAGE 23.

16. *warring successors:* on the death of Alexander a long and obscure struggle ensued between his various generals who had seized portions of his empire. Only

JULIUS CAESAR

two of these empires were permanent, that of Seleucus (Persia and Mesopotamia), and that of Ptolemy (Egypt).

24. *Arbela:* the third and decisive battle between Darius and Alexander on a plain in Syria (331 B.C.).

PAGE 26.

19. *Bucephalus:* so called because its head resembled that of an ox.

PAGE 28.

2. *Susa:* in what is now Iran, about 150 miles north of the Persian Gulf.

JULIUS CAESAR

PAGE 29.

4. *'the Julian Calendar':* see pages 62-3.

22. *Dante:* Dante Alighieri (1265-1321), the Italian poet (see note to page 140, below). The passage referred to is in the *Inferno*, xxxiv, 67.

24. *Shakespeare:* see pages 112-140. The play is of course *Julius Caesar*.

PAGE 30.

4. *patrician:* a Roman nobleman.

7. *It dominated:* see map opposite.

9. *Parthia:* the mountainous country south-east of the Caspian Sea.

10. *Carthage:* a city on the north coast of Africa, opposite Sicily, and mother of a great empire. It was finally burned by the Romans in 146 B.C.

25. *the Senate:* the state council of the elders of Rome.

28. *Sulla:* Lucius Cornelius Sulla (138-78 B.C.). For him the title of 'dictator' was revived and he was virtually Emperor of Rome.

28. *proscription:* a list of men declared to be outlaws and public enemies was exhibited in the Forum (see note to page 37, below), so starting a reign of terror.

NOTES

PAGE 32.

1. *Marius:* Caius Marius (157-86 B.C.). He was five times elected consul and hailed as the 'saviour of his country' for his victory over the nomadic hordes of the Cimbri and the Teutones.

27. *one of the great writers of prose:* his *De Bello Gallico*, an account of his own campaigns, written in the third person, is a classic historical work. See page 46.

PAGE 33.

15. *Rhodes:* an island off the coast of Asia Minor.

PAGE 34.

2. *demagogue:* popular agitator.

10. *Pompey:* Cneius Pompeius (106-48 B.C.). He was the ally of Sulla against Marius, and then cleared the western Mediterranean of pirates.

11. *Cicero:* Marcus Tullius Cicero (106-43 B.C.). Famous both as an orator and a writer of prose.

32. *Chief Pontiff:* Pontifex Maximus, the chief administrator of religious law.

PAGE 35.

3. *Crassus:* Marcus Licinius Crassus (c. 115-53 B.C.). He had been Pompey's fellow consul, but now opposed him.

PAGE 36.

3. *The Catilinian party was crushed:* Catiline himself fell in battle.

PAGE 37.

16. *the Forum:* the market place and place of assembly in Rome, adorned with temples and public buildings.

PAGE 38.

2. *Etruria:* the modern Tuscany, a province of Italy whence the Romans derived much of their civilization.

3. *the river Rubicon:* in north-east Italy, see map opposite page 30.

JULIUS CAESAR

3. *Cisalpine:* on this (the Roman) side of the Alps. Transalpine Gaul was beyond the Alps.

6. *Pyrenees:* the mountain-range dividing Gaul from Spain.

PAGE 39.

30. *the Helvetii:* a Celto-Germanic people inhabiting what is now Switzerland.

PAGE 40.

7. *Alsace:* a district in north-east Gaul.

PAGE 41.

21. *the Druid religion:* the Druids were so called after the Greek name for ' oak ', for their veneration of this tree ; their priests were interpreters of the gods, and supreme judges.

PAGE 42.

26. *piles:* heavy beams driven vertically into the bed of the river.

PAGE 43.

23. *the Narrow Seas:* the English Channel, and the Straits of Dover.

32. *North Foreland:* the extreme promontory of Kent.

32. *Deal:* a town on the Kent coast, south of the North Foreland.

PAGE 45.

12. *Vercingetorix:* chief of the Arveni.

17. *commissariat:* department for the supply of food.

PAGE 47.

22. *the Parthians:* a people of Scythian origin who lived south-east of the Caspian Sea.

24. *triumvirs:* a political alliance of three men, such as that of Caesar, Pompey and Crassus, was called a triumvirate.

NOTES

Page 48.

   14. *proconsul:* governor of a province.

Page 49.

   24. *Ravenna:* a city on the Adriatic.
   29. *levies:* enrolments of men for war.

Page 50.

   17. *crossed the Rubicon:* this has since become a stock phrase for the making of an irrevocable decision.
   29. *Capua:* a prosperous city in Southern Italy.

Page 54.

   17. *Virgil's tremendous line:* the *Aeneid*, bk. VI, l. 853.

Page 55.

   23. *Durazzo:* a seaport on the Adriatic.

Page 56.

   5. *Mount Olympus:* a lofty mountain dividing Greece from Macedon, and regarded as the home of the Gods.
   6. *Thermopylae:* a narrow pass between Mount Oeta and the Maliac Gulf.
   13. *cohorts:* divisions of the Roman army.
   27. *obelisk:* it was brought to London in 1878, and has nothing to do with Cleopatra.

Page 57.

   10. *Cleopatra:* eldest daughter of Ptolemy Auletes, King of Egypt, she lived from 68-30 B.C.

Page 59.

   3. *Cato:* Marcus Porcius Cato, the republican.
   9. *Labienus:* He was one of the first to desert Caesar on the outbreak of the civil war, and was killed at Munden in 45 B.C.
   12. *Utica:* an ancient Tyrian colony in North Africa.

CHARLEMAGNE

PAGE 60.

4. *Sextus Pompey:* (75-35 B.C.) He finally fled into Asia Minor where he was captured and executed.

5. *guerilla warfare:* irregular warfare waged by small bodies acting independently.

29. *lictors:* officers attending Roman consul and dictator bearing fasces (bundles of rods with an axe in the middle).

CHARLEMAGNE

PAGE 66.

10. *who still sits somewhere:* see pages 85-6.
19. *the last stand of Roland:* see pages 74-5.
25. *Roncesvalles:* a valley in the Western Pyrenees.

PAGE 69.

1. *greatest child:* Julius Caesar.
21. *Pepin:* named 'the short'. He reigned from A.D. 751-768.

PAGE 70.

30. *Saxons:* a warlike race from North Germany, subdued by Charlemagne after many fierce conflicts.

31. *Lombards:* a people deriving their name from the German Langobardi. They established a kingdom in North Italy which lasted from 568 to 774.

31. *Saracens:* a name given to the first disciples of Mahomet, who subdued a great part of Asia, Africa, and Europe. They conquered Spain in 711 onwards, and established the Caliphate of Cordova. See page 73.

PAGE 71.

1. *Avars:* barbarians who ravaged the Eastern Empire in the sixth and seventh centuries; subdued by Charlemagne after an eight years' war.

21. *thurifers:* incense-bearers.

NOTES

PAGE 73.

13. *Tunis:* in north Africa near the site of Carthage.

30. *Barcelona:* a town on the north-east coast of Spain.

PAGE 74.

3. *Pampeluna:* north-east Spain.

4. *the Basques:* an independent people in north-east Spain.

4. *Saragossa:* north-east Spain.

20. *Archbishop Turpin:* (d. *c.* 800) Archbishop of Rheims. According to one version he died among the last of the heroes at Roncesvalles.

24. *Lord Ganelon:* Count of Mayence. He figures in Dante's *Inferno,* xxxii, 122.

PAGE 75.

7. *Mordred:* nephew of King Arthur. He traitorously seized the kingdom and Queen Guinevere during Arthur's absence, and was killed by Arthur in the final battle in Cornwall.

PAGE 79.

5. *basilica:* a collonaded building used as a royal palace or a church.

7. *the tomb of the Apostle:* St. Peter. The church was built on the traditional place of his crucifixion, and is the central church of the Roman Catholic Faith.

PAGE 80.

31. *in fief:* in fee.

PAGE 81.

7. *the Empress Irene:* (752-803). She became sole ruler of the Empire on her husband's death. Her son, Constantine VI, later proclaimed emperor in her stead, was seized and beheaded at her command.

JOAN OF ARC

26. *Haroun-al-Raschid:* (763-809), caliph of Bagdad, known best to Europeans from the tales about him in the *Arabian Nights.* His rule extended from India to Africa.

PAGE 82.

10. *bigots:* persons who attach disproportionate weight to some creed or view.

21. *candelabra:* large branched candlesticks.

PAGE 83.

9. *Alcuin:* (735-804), theologian and man of letters.

PAGE 85.

17. *Scandinavia:* the ancient name of Sweden, Norway, and a great part of Denmark.

27. *septuagenarian:* of seventy years of age.

PAGE 86.

3. *paladins:* the twelve peers of Charlemagne's court, of whom the Count Palatine was the chief.

JOAN OF ARC

PAGE 88.

27. *she, Julius Caesar, and Cleopatra:* she is the heroine of George Bernard Shaw's *St. Joan* (1923), and anything but the heroine of Shakespeare's *Henry VI,* Part I. Caesar and Cleopatra are of course from Shakespeare's *Julius Caesar* and *Anthony and Cleopatra* respectively and occur together in Shaw's *Caesar and Cleopatra* (1898).

32. *Henry IV:* (1367-1413). He deposed and succeeded Richard II in 1399.

PAGE 89.

2. *Henry V:* (1387-1422). He commanded the victorious English army at Agincourt in 1415, and laid

NOTES

the foundations of a national navy and of military, international and maritime law.

14. *the Black Death:* the Great Pestilence or Oriental Plague, which devastated most countries of Europe in the fourteenth century.

21. *the baby Henry VI:* (1421-1471). He became King of England when only nine months old.

22. *the Duke of Bedford:* John of Lancaster, Duke of Bedford (1389-1435).

PAGE 91.

1. *Thomas the Rhymer:* Thomas of Erceldoune (*fl.* 1220?-1297?), Scottish seer and poet.

PAGE 92.

28. *St. Margaret:* virgin and martyr. Daughter of a pagan priest of Antioch.

PAGE 93.

1. *St. Catherine:* St. Catherine of Alexandria, virgin and martyr. A most popular saint in the Middle Ages. She was executed by the Emperor Maximinus.

PAGE 96.

6. *Chinon:* a town of western France, south-west of Tours.

PAGE 98.

17. *catechized:* put a series of questions to.

PAGE 100.

24. *Count de Dunois:* (1403-1468), commonly called 'the Bastard of Orleans'.

PAGE 101.

13. *Blois:* a town thirty-five miles south-west of Orleans.

PAGE 102.

13. *Rheims:* The kings of France were crowned here because Clovis, the founder of the French monarchy, was baptized here.

WILLIAM SHAKESPEARE

PAGE 105.

30. *Compiegne:* a city north of Paris.

PAGE 106.

20. *my lord of Luxembourg:* Jean de **Luxembourg** (d. 1440).

PAGE 107.

12. *Richard I:* 'Coeur de Lion', King of England, 1157-99.

14. *Charles Duke of Orleans:* (1391-1465). He was taken prisoner by the English at Agincourt and ransomed after twenty-five years easy captivity.

29. *the Bishop of Beauvais:* Peter Cauchon (d. **1442**).

PAGE 108.

14. *the Earl of Warwick:* Richard de Beauchamp, Earl of Warwick (1382-1439).

WILLIAM SHAKESPEARE

PAGE 113.

10. *bailiff:* a kind of mayor or sheriff.
20. *burgess:* citizen with full rights.

PAGE 114.

12. *Ovid:* Publius Ovidius Naso (43 B.C.-A.D. 18?), the Roman elegiac poet.

12. *Ben Jonson:* (1572-1637), see page 136.

PAGE 116.

2. *Sir Edmund Chambers:* (b. 1866), celebrated Elizabethan scholar; his *William Shakespeare; the facts and problems* (1930) is the most authoritative Shakespearean biography.

21. *Cotswold:* the Cotswolds are a range of hills in the west midlands of England.

30. *the Armada:* the enormous fleet collected and equipped by Philip II of Spain in 1588 for the subjugation

NOTES

of England. It was defeated in the English Channel and afterwards dispersed and partly destroyed by storms.

PAGE 117.

2. *Robert Greene:* (1560?-1592). The most famous of his five plays is *Friar Bacon and Friar Bungay*, acted in 1594.

31. *Christopher Marlowe:* (1564-1593), author of *Dr. Faustus, The Jew of Malta, Edward II, Tamburlaine*, etc.

PAGE 118.

30. *a later story:* the first written evidence for it is in 1748, when it is attributed to Sir William Davenant.

PAGE 119.

26. *Henry Chettle:* (d. 1607?), besides being a publisher was author and part author of several plays.

PAGE 120.

9. *conceits:* products of the imagination.

PAGE 121.

3. *the Earl of Southampton:* Henry Wriothesley, third Earl of Southampton (1573-1624). He was condemned to death for complicity in the Essex rebellion, the sentence commuted, and he himself released by James I.

8. *Earl of Essex:* Robert Devereux, second Earl of Essex (1566-1601). He was executed for treason after attempting to raise a rebellion in the City.

25. *William Kempe:* a well-known comic actor. He once danced a morris-dance from London to Norwich.

26. *Richard Burbage:* (1567?-1619), an actor of chief parts in plays by Shakespeare and Ben Jonson. He excelled in tragedy.

27. *Lord Chamberlain:* one of the three departmental heads of the Royal Household. He was responsible for all Court entertainments.

31. *St. Stephen's Day:* 26th December.

WILLIAM SHAKESPEARE

31. *Innocents' Day:* (Or Childermas), the 28th December. In memory of the slaughter of the Holy Innocents (Matthew ii).

PAGE 122.

1. *Apocryphal stories:* stories on doubtful authority.

4. *Falstaff:* Sir John Falstaff in Shakespeare's *Henry IV*. A fat, witty, good-humoured old knight, self-indulgent, and a resourceful braggart. The Falstaff of *Merry Wives of Windsor* is a far shallower and sorrier character.

15. *that very time . . . :* A *Midsummer-Night's Dream*, II. i. 155.

18. *vestal:* a virgin, dedicated to the service of the Roman goddess Vesta, the goddess of Fire.

23. *votaress:* maiden vowed to the service of Diana. Diana was goddess both of the moon and of virginity, and Elizabeth is her votaress.

24. *fancy-free:* free from the power of love.

PAGE 124.

18. *Abraham Cowley:* (1618-67). His reputation was considerable in his own day.

20. *Richard Crashaw:* (1612?-49). His principal poetic work was the *Steps to the Temple*, a collection of religious poems showing great devotional ecstasy.

PAGE 127.

23. *a fine house and garden:* it was called New Place.

PAGE 128.

7. *a corner:* a combination to raise the price of a commodity by securing a monopoly.

15. *Lord Burleigh:* William Cecil, Lord Burleigh (1520-98), Queen Elizabeth's chief minister.

26. *the Earl of Essex:* see note to page 121 above.

NOTES

PAGE 129.

12. *tithes:* taxes of one-tenth part of annual proceeds of land.

14. *dog-Latin:* incorrect or mongrel Latin.

PAGE 130.

3. *Carter Lane:* in the City of London, between St. Paul's and the Thames.

11. *Evesham:* a town in Worcestershire.

28. *apothecary:* druggist, chemist.

PAGE 131.

3. *Bishopsgate:* the principal north gate of the ancient city of London.

7. *Southwark:* the district south of the Thames near London Bridge. Here were most of the theatres, bear-gardens, etc.

31. *Globe Theatre:* erected in 1598 in Southwark. It was an octagonal building, said to hold 1,200 spectators.

PAGE 132.

2. *Richard II:* this play was reckoned particularly apt as offering the spectacle of the deposition of a monarch.

PAGE 133.

3. *Essex House:* stood in the Strand, with its garden running down to the river Thames.

12. *Cecil:* Robert Cecil (1563?-1612), son of Lord Burleigh, and his father's successor as Elizabeth's chief minister.

16. *James I:* James VI of Scotland came to the English throne as James I, on the death of Elizabeth in 1603.

PAGE 134.

2. *the King's Men:* see below.

2. *King Lear . . . Othello: King Lear* deals with the sufferings of an old king, driven out of doors and maddened

WILLIAM SHAKESPEARE

by ill-treatment; *Othello* with the strangling of a wife by her jealous husband.

13. *Sierra Leone:* on the coast of West Africa.

PAGE 135.

3. *Castile:* a kingdom in Central Spain.

6. *Lady Pembroke:* (1561-1621), sister of Sir Philip Sidney, mother of the Earl of Pembroke, and subject of a famous epitaph by William Browne.

7. *Sir Walter Raleigh:* (1552?-1618), the famous seaman, poet and historian. He was imprisoned in the Tower of London from 1603 to 1616, released to go on an expedition in search of gold, and, when the venture failed, executed on the demand of the Spanish ambassador.

9. *Salisbury:* in Wiltshire.

16. ' *two-fold balls and treble sceptres carry* ' : *Macbeth*, IV. i. 121. Macbeth is shown a vision of the future kings of Scotland. This line was Shakespeare's compliment to James I.

28. *Dead shepherd . . .: As You Like It*, III. v. 81 ; saw = saying, proverb.

PAGE 136.

4. (*as has been said*) : page 114.

7. *as Shakespeare did in the Sonnets:* e.g. Sonnets, 17, 19, 55, 60, 63, 65.

22. *the Ghost:* the first written evidence we have of this is in 1709.

22. *Adam:* Recorded in 1774, from the hearsay of an old Stratford countryman.

PAGE 137.

1. *Huguenot:* a member of the French Reformed Church.

5. *John Milton:* (1608-74) one of the greatest English poets; author of *Paradise Lost*.

NOTES

PAGE 138.

7. *depose:* swear on oath.

14. *New Place:* see page 127.

29. *sack:* kinds of white wine.

PAGE 139.

10. *Burbadge:* see note to page 121 above.

11. *Heminges . . . Condell:* John Hemmings (d. 1630), and Henry Condell (d. 1627); these fellow actors edited the First Folio of Shakespeare's plays (1623).

21. *chattels:* movable possessions.

23. *entailed:* settled so that it cannot be bequeathed at pleasure.

28. *Michael Drayton:* (1563-1631), poet. His most famous work was a topographical poem *Polyolbion.*

PAGE 140.

16. *Dante's Divine Comedy:* The *Divina Commedia* was the masterpiece of Dante Alighieri (1265-1321), the great Italian poet. It comprises the *Inferno*, the *Purgatorio*, and the *Paradiso*.

18. *Aeneid of Virgil:* a poem recounting the adventures of Aeneas from the fall of Troy, and glorifying the Roman Empire, by P. Virgilius Maro (70-19 B.C.) the Roman poet.

VOLTAIRE

PAGE 141.

1. *Robert Browning:* (1812-89). The poem was *The Ring and the Book* (1868-9).

27. *the Duke of St. Simon:* (1675-1755) author of *Mémoires*, famous for the vivid picture they give of the courts of Louis XIV and the Regent d'Orléans.

PAGE 142.

7. *the Academy:* (*l'Académie Française*) founded by Cardinal Richelieu in 1635; essentially a literary academy.

VOLTAIRE

19. *Shakespeare . . . the Earl of Southampton:* see page 121.

PAGE 143.

3. *Marquis de Saint Ange:* Louis de Caumarthin, Marquis de Saint Ange.

12. *Madame de Maintenon:* (1635-1719), wife of the French poet Scarron. After her husband's death she was charged with the education of the children of Louis XIV.

16. *Louis XV:* (1710-1774). He was five years old when Louis XIV died.

21. *the Bastille:* a castle built in 1369 for the defence of Paris, and afterwards used as a state prison. Pulled down by the populace in 1789.

PAGE 144.

20. *L'Henriade:* published in 1723.

PAGE 147.

4. *Jesuits:* the Society of Jesus, founded by St. Ignatius Loyola (1491-1556), bound by vows of chastity, poverty, obedience, and submission to the Pope.

4. *Frederick of Prussia:* Friedrich II (1712-86).

PAGE 149.

9. *William Congreve:* (1670-1729), one of the greatest writers of English comedy.

18. *Charles XII of Sweden:* reigned from 1682-1718; a great military commander, after victories in Poland and Russia, he was defeated at Poltava and lost all his conquests.

28. *Sir Isaac Newton:* (1642-1727), the philosopher who made important discoveries in many branches of science and mathematics, and was President of the Royal Society for twenty-five years.

PAGE 150.

31. *Te Deums:* the *Te Deum*, a Latin hymn of praise, of ancient origin, so called from its opening words.

NOTES

PAGE 151.

4. *Byron:* George Gordon, Lord Byron (1788-1824).

6. *The one was fire . . .: Childe Harold's Pilgrimage,* III, 986-994.

11. *The Proteus of their talents:* versatile. Proteus was the sea-deity, who could assume many shapes.

12. *as the wind:* St. John iii. 8.

PAGE 152.

15. *Madame du Chatelet:* Emilie de Breteuil, marquise du Chatelet. She died in 1749.

PAGE 153.

9. *the Empress of Russia:* Catherine II (1762-96). She was the friend of Voltaire, and was influenced by his writings.

PAGE 154.

7. *Potsdam:* near Berlin. The palace of *Sans Souci* owed its embellishments to Frederick.

PAGE 155.

5. *Maupertuis:* Pierre Louis Moreau de Maupertuis (1698-1759).

PAGE 157.

23. '*Four soldiers fired . . .*': *Candide*, chapter xxiii. The execution referred to was that of Admiral Byng in 1757 for neglect of duty.

PAGE 159.

10. *Toulouse:* a city in the south of France.

PAGE 162.

15. *Benjamin Franklin:* (1706-90). Printer and diplomat. As agent for the American colonies he first strove to avert the breach between them and Great Britain, but afterwards negotiated the alliance between them and France.

20. *His last play:* this was *Irène*.

JOHN WESLEY

PAGE 164.

5. *La Barre:* the Chevalier de la Barre was executed in 1765 for mutilating a crucifix. Among his possessions were found many pamphlets by Voltaire, who was threatened in consequence.

5. *Sirven:* this was similar to the Calas case, except that the Sirven family fled before they could be arrested. It was nine years before they were acquitted.

5. *Montbailly:* a case of judicial error like those of Calas and Sirven.

JOHN WESLEY

PAGE 165.

25. *William Law:* (1686-1761). The book that influenced Wesley was his *Serious Call to a Devout and Holy Life* (1729).

PAGE 166.

25.' *the Calas case:* see pages 159-61.

PAGE 167.

26. *Charles:* Charles Wesley (1707-88). He founded the 'methodist' society to which John Wesley and George Whitefield belonged and is remembered as the composer of many hymns.

PAGE 168.

16. *Robinson Crusoe:* the world-famous novel of adventure on an uninhabited island by Daniel Defoe, published in 1719.

PAGE 169.

14. *George Whitefield:* (1714-70). His followers and those of Wesley separated and formed rival parties.

PAGE 170.

16. *General Oglethorpe:* James Edward Oglethorpe (1698-1795).

NOTES

23. *Moravian Brethren:* a Protestant sect founded early in the eighteenth century in Saxony, by emigrants from Moravia, an Austrian province. It obtained many adherents from England and the American colonies.

PAGE 172.

26. *studying Newton:* see note to page 149 above.

31. *Martin Luther:* (1483-1546), the leader of the Reformation in Germany.

PAGE 173.

19. *Newman:* John Henry Newman (1801-90).

29. *corollary:* natural consequence, self-evident inference.

PAGE 174.

16. *Samuel:* Samuel Wesley, the younger (1691-1739). He became a schoolmaster.

PAGE 175.

8. *Archimides:* (287-212 B.C.) famous mathematician of Syracuse, to whom many great scientific discoveries are credited.

PAGE 176.

23. '*The Spirit of the Lord* . . .': Isaiah lxi. 1-2.

PAGE 181.

8. *Horace Walpole:* Fourth Earl of Orford (1771-97), established his printing press at Strawberry Hill, near Twickenham. His literary reputation rests on his interesting letters.

9. *Beau Nash:* Richard Nash (1674-1762). Established the Assembly Rooms at Bath, drew up a code of etiquette and dress, and became the unquestioned autocrat of society.

26. *Pump-room:* the room where the curing waters were drunk, and there was music and dancing.

JOHN WESLEY

PAGE 182.

7. *Southey's Life of Wesley:* Robert Southey (1774-1843), Poet Laureate, published this biography in 1830. It is one of the best biographies in the language.

PAGE 183.

17. *Wednesbury:* a town in Staffordshire.

PAGE 184.

2. *the Old Pretender:* James Francis Edward Stuart (1688-1766), son of the exiled James II. Pretender here means one who makes pretensions; a claimant.

3. *Charles Edward:* (1720-88), the young Pretender, son of the above.

9. *Jacobites:* partisans of the Stuarts after the Revolution of 1688, from *Jacobus*, Latin for James.

PAGE 186.

18. *dogma:* doctrine or system of doctrine, as defined by authority.

PAGE 187.

29. *John Calvin:* (1509-64) the great French theological reformer. He was the originator of the dogma of Scottish Presbyterianism.

PAGE 188.

2. *ancient Roman walls:* the walls erected by Agricola, Hadrian, and Septimus Severus to defend Britain from the Picts and the Scots.

20. *the American Revolution:* the breaking-away of the American colonies from England. Great Britain recognized their independence in 1783.

27. *Dr. Johnson:* (1709-84) famous English man of letters and compiler of the *English Dictionary* (1755).

PAGE 189.

1. *Mrs. Thrale:* (1741-1821) the friend of Dr. Johnson and wife of a wealthy brewer.

NOTES

1. *Streatham:* then a village seven miles south of London, now a densely populated suburb.

9. *Boswell:* James Boswell (1740-95); the friend and biographer of Johnson. Boswell's *Life of Johnson* is one of the most successful and intimate biographies ever written.

PAGE 191.

24. *Lambeth:* the district south of the Thames from Westminster Bridge.

25. *Voltaire had similarly suffered:* see page 163.

www.ingramcontent.com/pod-product-compliance
Lightning Source LLC
Chambersburg PA
CBHW022059160426
43198CB00008B/282